ROCKS, DIRT, WORMS & WEEDS

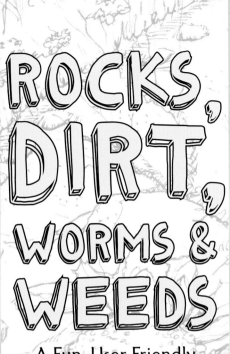

ROCKS, DIRT, WORMS & WEEDS

A Fun, User-Friendly,
Illustrated Guide to
Creating a Vegetable or
Flower Garden
with Your Kids

JEFF HUTTON

Skyhorse Publishing

To my wife, Diane . . .
And to the smaller gardeners in our life:
Riley, Dylan, Molly, Colby, Chase, and Sienna

Acknowledgments: This would not have been possible without the wonderful collaboration of my editor, Lilly Golden, and everyone at Skyhorse who helped imagine this book.

Skyhorse Publishing books may be purchased in bulk at special discounts for sales promotion, corporate gifts, fund-raising, or educational purposes. Special editions can also be created to specifications. For details, contact the Special Sales Department, Skyhorse Publishing, 307 West 36th Street, 11th Floor, New York, NY 10018 or info@skyhorsepublishing.com.

Skyhorse® and Skyhorse Publishing® are registered trademarks of Skyhorse Publishing, Inc.®, a Delaware corporation.

Visit our website at www.skyhorsepublishing.com.

10 9 8 7 6 5 4 3 2 1

Library of Congress Cataloging-in-Publication Data
Hutton, Jeff.
 Rocks, dirt, worms & weeds : a fun, user-friendly illustrated guide to creating a vegetable or flower garden with your kids / Jeff Hutton.
     p. cm.
 Rocks, dirt, worms and weeds
 ISBN 978-1-61608-722-7 (pbk. : alk. paper)
1. Gardening. I. Title. II. Title: Rocks, dirt, worms and weeds.
SB453.H88 2012
635--dc23

2011052505

Printed in China

CONTENTS

Part One: Spring

1. GETTING DIRTY—ALL ABOUT SOIL AND MORE   3

Activities include: • Simple Soil Sample Kit
• Decorating Your Own Garden Tool Box • Finding North
• Simple Rain Gauge • Another Type of Rain Gauge

2. STARTING SEEDS INDOORS AND OTHER
INDOOR GARDENING PROJECTS   11

Activities include: • Starting Seeds in Peat Pot Kits or Trays

• Egg Carton Gardens and "Egg"cellent Gifts
• Decorating Clay Pots
• How to Build a Simple Cold Frame
• Simple Window Gardens
• Hairy Man • Mini Herb Garden

3. GROWING A VEGETABLE GARDEN   27

Activities include: • Planning the Garden
• Building Simple Raised Beds • Fancy Plant Markers

• Container Tomato Garden
• Something Sour: Growing and Making Pickles
• A Popcorn Garden • An Amazing Maize Maze
• A Salsa Garden • Strawberry Pots • Garden Journal

4. WORMS AND OTHER FRIENDS   47

Activities include: • Worm Bin • Painting Ladybug Rocks

Part Two: Summer

5. FUN WITH FLOWERS   57

Activities include: • Planting a Sunflower Maze

• Keep a Sunflower Journal

• Making Pressed Flowers—Preserving Some of Your Summer

6. WEEDS AND OTHER WONDERS   67

7. "FLYING FLOWERS": BUTTERFLIES AND BUTTERFLY GARDENS   73

Activities include: • Creating a Butterfly Garden

• Caterpillar Bowls • Butterfly Journals

8. GARDENING IS FOR THE BIRDS   81

Activities include: • How to Make Two Simple Bird Feeders

• Do It with Suet • How to Build a Simple Birdhouse • Bird Journals

9. WATER, WATER EVERYWHERE   89

Activities include: • Setting Up a Rain Barrel • Rain Chain

• Making Your Own Green Roof

10. STEPPING STONES, ROCK GARDENING,
AND OTHER OUTDOOR ART   97

Activities include: • How to Make Your Stepping Stone

• Stone Wreath • Be a Rock Artist

• The Art of Stick Weaving • Grapevine Wreaths

• Painting on Slate or Bluestone • Painting on Wood

Part Three: Fall

11. GREAT PUMPKINS AND MORE FALL HARVEST FUN   **111**

Activities include: • Pumpkin Carving

• Tasty Roasted Pumpkin Seeds

• Saving Pumpkin Seeds for Next Year's Garden

• Painting Gourds

12. COLD PEAS AND ROTTEN POTATOES: THE JOYS OF COMPOST   **119**

Activities include: • Making Your Own Simple Compost Bin

Part Four: Winter

13. TO SNOW AND BEYOND   **125**

Activities include: • Snow Measuring Sticks • Wind Sock

• Make Your Own Paper • Adding Decorations

14. WHAT GOES AROUND COMES AROUND   **135**

Part One:

Spring

Over many years,
large earth masses
have eroded and
added to the
earth's surface
of healthy soil.

GETTING DIRTY—ALL ABOUT SOIL AND MORE

Dirt—or top soil, as we gardeners like to call it—is the foundation of everything we grow. It's really one of the foundations of life itself. It allows us to grow food crops like vegetables and fruit, grains, herbs, and plants used for medicines. It supports the plants that clean the air through their own living process and allows the growth of roots and foliage (or leaves), which slow down the ongoing process of **erosion**[1]. And remember that cows eat grass and grains that grow in our good soil and then they give us milk . . . and even ice cream.

IT'S ALIVE! Top soil is alive, and that's what makes it so important. Soil is a product of large rocks slowly breaking down into smaller rocks and finally into tiny particles. A long time ago, when the earth was young, big blocks of ice called glaciers moved across its surface and dragged rocks and other stuff with it. Over the years the huge boul-

---

1   Erosion: the process in which something is worn down into smaller particles

ders broke down slowly into smaller rocks. They bumped and broke until they became smaller and smaller. Animals and other living things eventually died and became part of the earth's top layer. Little plants struggled to grow, and when they died they became part of this top layer too. Living things contribute what we call "organic" matter to the earth's surface. On a smaller scale this goes on every day to continue a healthy cycle.

Ground actually moves and shifts with different temperatures. When it gets really cold, the ground freezes and rocks move upward. The **friction**[2] of this movement wears the rock down too. Friction actually produces heat as well. Rub your hands together a few times. You can feel the warmth. Over a lot of years wind and rain and friction wore the big rocks down more—even rolled them with strong wind and ground that shifted with changing temperatures and weather.

Old leaves and other plants full of little **microbes**[3] (a fancy word for tiny living things) fall to the ground and decay, adding to the dirt. Insects and other little creatures tunnel though, exchange air, allow for the movement of water, and finally complete their life cycles, becoming part of the world of soil and the continuing cycle of nature. Other plants, such as moss, grow in the decaying environment, adding even more nutrients, and help turn "dirt" to soil. It's like a big soup of different ingredients—all very important to the final recipe.

This living soil is all around us.

Healthy soil is always changing, from a long time ago when the rock masses were being worn down to pebbles and smaller particles, and even now, in your backyard, as leaves and flowers fall and bugs settle into the ground, becoming part of the healthy mix, ready to grow your garden.

---

2   Friction: energy caused by the rubbing of two things together
3   Microbe: a really small living thing that you need to view through a microscope

So let's get out into the yard and garden and check out what's in our top soil.

SIMPLE SOIL SAMPLE

Exploring below the surface

 # Simple Soil Sample Kit

Take an empty plastic soda bottle and cut the bottom off. Twist the bottle into a soft part of the yard or garden on a slightly damp day. Flip it upside down and you'll end up with a column sample of the top soil. You can tell by the color if it's dark and rich or light and sandy. Geologists and other professionals do this on a larger scale: these are called core samples.

If it falls apart and spills out, you must have fairly sandy soil. If it sticks together, it usually contains more clay. If you have very sandy soil, you can improve it by adding organic material like **compost**[4] or peat moss. Peat moss is really just a mass of decayed leaves and plants that form in low wetlands called bogs. It is rich with nutrients and organic material. Compost is something we'll learn about in Chapter 12. (You can jump ahead to learn all

---

4   Compost: a mixture of decaying organic material, such as food scraps; a way to recycle food and paper wastes

about it if you like!) If your soil clumps together, you may need to improve drainage by adding sand or fine gravel.

Remember, this is a simple beginner's test. It's a good way to gain an understanding of top soil. You can take samples from different parts of the yard to compare. But you can also get soil kits from a local agricultural extension center if you want more information. Many of these places will offer a free scientific evaluation of your garden soil.

Gardening always involves exploration and discovery. One of the important "discoveries" of gardening is finding how much you get in return for your efforts. And once they get started, many people become lifetime gardeners. It's a pastime that almost always produces results.

  Decorating Your Own Garden Tool Box

Keeping your own tools and adding to your collection can be a lot of fun. Find an old wooden box, like the kind wine bottles or fruit come in. You can paint it or decorate it in some way to give it your own style. Gardening should be a creative activity and your garden can reflect your own personality. Use the garden box to hold your garden tools, gloves, seed packets, and anything else you collect that may be useful.

Customize your box and make it your own. Keep your tools clean and easy to find.

A Start-up Kit for Young Gardeners:

Here are a few tools that will come in handy:

A hand trowel

A hand cultivator

Garden gloves

A small rake

A small shovel

Pants or shorts you don't mind getting dirty

Old sneakers or rubber gardening shoes

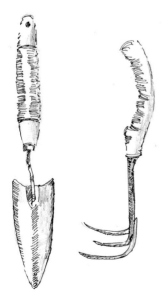

Hand trowel
and cultivator

Choose sturdy and comfortable shoes
that you don't mind getting dirty.

Finding North

Knowing where north is becomes very important when you're planning a landscape or garden. Ideally, you want your garden to face south. We know the sun shining from the south is the warmest, and the coldest wind comes from the north. Although not precise, the simplest way to find north is to stand out in your yard in the early morning. If you stand up straight and extend your right arm to the sun while it is still low and rising in the sky, and then extend your left arm in the opposite direction forming a "T," you'll

be facing north. Your nose will point north if you're facing straight ahead.

Remember, if you're facing north, south is right behind you.

Cold nose: if you are pointing east with your right hand and looking straight ahead, your nose should be pointing north.

Simple Rain Gauge

Gardens need water. The easiest way for a garden to get water is from rain. An average of an inch per week is enough to grow most crops and flowers. Do you get enough rain where you live? You can find out. Choose an open area in the yard, not too far from the house but away from the edges of the roof. Take a large clear plastic container (try a large pretzel or popcorn container) and measure out inches and then break those spaces down to half inches. Mark these lines clearly with a permanent marker or paint. Label each

line as a measurement on a ruler. Cover the container with some kind of screen so leaves don't get in, but water from the rain will. Measure the screen larger than the hole at the top of the container, cut the screen, and fold it over the top. Find some big rubber bands or electrical tape to secure it. Place it somewhere you can check it easily.

Activity Another Type of Rain Gauge

Pick an open space in the yard. Try finding a spot that you can see from a window in the house. Instead of marking the outside of the container with measurements, make a slit in the center of the screen top, and carefully push a plastic or wooden ruler down until it hits the bottom of the container. You should be able to read the measurements from each rainfall on the ruler at the center. If you don't have a ruler, make your own. Find a way to measure inches and half-inches along a piece of wood or plastic and mark it with a waterproof magic marker or paint. After a rainstorm, see how high the water has come on the ruler. Then, empty the container and clean it out so you can see it easily when the next storm comes through.

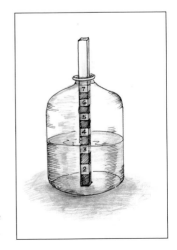

Find a spot to place the rain gauge so that you can see it from a window.

STARTING SEEDS INDOORS AND OTHER INDOOR GARDENING PROJECTS

What's a seed? Actually, it's a baby plant encased in a kind of shell. There are lots of different kinds of seeds. As plants grow they produce new seeds, so they continue to thrive from season to season.

Most people, kids and adults alike, enjoy gardening and gardens because of the color and fragrance produced by the flower, foliage (leaves), and delicious vegetables. Wonderful fruits, nuts, and berries also come from gardens. These are the results of planning and effort. But just as the party starts with the first phone call, the garden starts with the first seed and an idea of where you might plant it.

The coldest part of the winter—January and February—is a great time to start thinking about what you want to grow. As a family you

This might be where we're heading . . .

. . . but this is where we start!!!!

should order a seed catalog. The large companies, such as Burpee, provide beautiful color catalogs featuring all of the plants you can grow from seed. Get on the mailing list and your family will receive these every winter. These catalogs are free and filled with pictures of flowers or vegetables, with information on how much sun and room a plant needs to grow. And the best thing is they arrive in the mail (or online) when the snow might still be on the ground and your garden is just a gleam in your eye.

To understand which plants will do well where you live, consult the web page for the United States National Arboretum/USDA Plant Hardiness Zone Map or your local library.

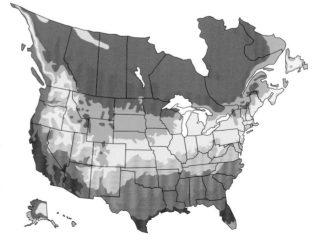

A HEAD START: STARTING SEEDS INDOORS.

In colder climates, you can get a head start in late March or April by planting your seeds indoors. Many annual flowers and vegetable plants won't survive the frost on a cold night, so getting them started indoors lets you begin in the spring before the ground is even thawed. Many areas of the southern United States enjoy year-round gardening. But in the north, it's mid-May before you're safe to set plants outside—usually after the last full moon in May.

The first thing you need is a sunny window with a windowsill or a nearby table. This will become your indoor garden spot.

This is how to find a window with southern exposure: you must first determine on what side of the house you first see the sun in the morning. That's the eastern exposure, because the sun always rises in the east. Where's the last place you see the sun? That's the west. That's the direction in which the sun sets. What's the hottest, sunniest part of the yard in the summer? That would be the south-facing or southern exposure.

Do you have a basement with a sunny window in your house? That's one of the best places. If it's *too* sunny or *too* hot the plant will grow *too* fast and will become what gardeners call "leggy." No, this doesn't mean the plants grow legs and get up and walk away. What it does mean is the foliage and the stems will grow too fast and be weak and top-heavy.

Long "legs" mean your plants are stretching toward the sun.

13

Start simple: If this is your first time, start simple. Find an old wooden crate, like the type that clementines come in. Get two dozen two- or three-inch peat pots. Peat pots are little plant pots made of organic material and are usually available in sleeves of a dozen or more. They come in both round and square shapes. You can fill the pots with a **starter mix** (also called potting soil or potting mix, but it goes by other names as well) and tap the mix down gently with your fingers or your knuckles to get rid of any air pockets. Plant the seeds just below the surface according to the directions on the seed packet. Be careful when you open the packets. Some of these seeds are very tiny. But even the smallest ones produce wonderful plants.

Sowing seeds: This is just a fancy way of saying we're putting seeds in soil. The depth you should plant depends on the kind of seed you're planting. For most, the best way to start inside is to press your finger into the soil just past your fingernail. The little hole you've created should be about perfect for the seed. Drop a seed in the hole and then take a little bit of extra soil and fill in the hole. Press down gently on the surface of the soil. Carefully pour a little warm water on the surface and watch it soak in, or place the pot in a tray of water and let it soak in from the bottom.

Place your crate of peat pots on a plastic, metal, or foil tray or baking dish to catch the excess water when you water your seeds. Place the tray in a sunny, south-facing window. The great thing about starting plants in these peat pots is that when it's time to plant the young plants in your garden, you can plant the whole thing right in the ground—peat pot and all. The peat pot decomposes and just adds to the "good dirt." And this way you won't disturb the young root system when planting.

Starter Mix: Soil That's Not Really Soil

As much as we've already talked about how wonderful good top soil is in our gardens and landscape, it's not so good for starting plants or growing plants indoors. The air inside your house, or even a greenhouse, remains kind of still. And soil, when it's not dried by full sun and wind (moving air), can stay too wet. So there are mixtures sold that have a combination of ingredients that keep them very light but full of good food (nutrients) for the plants. Sometimes called **potting soil**, **planting mix**[5], or **starter mix**[6], this can be easily found in stores and nurseries. It should always be very light so it doesn't hold the water too long. If the soil stays too wet, the seeds or the plant roots might rot.

NOTE: One way to avoid things going wrong because of too much moisture is to spray the soil and plant with a baking soda mix. Try a teaspoon per pint of water mixed in a spray bottle and apply it once per week while you're growing indoors. Apply it both to the plant and to the surface of the soil. This can help keep the leaves from getting mold or fungus and prevent "damping off," a term for when the stem gets weak at the soil's surface.

---

5   Potting soil or planting mix: a special mix of soil to keep plants from staying too wet in pots
6   Starter mix: a mixture of soil and other ingredients especially formed to encourage growth of young seedlings

Starting Seeds in Peat Pot Kits or Trays

Another way to get started is to purchase starter kits. These usually include a planting tray that looks like a big ice cube tray, some soil mix, or even a pellet that expands when it gets wet. Some kits have a clear plastic top, so you're really forming your own miniature greenhouse. You will need to carefully pull the seedlings from the plastic pockets when you're ready to plant.

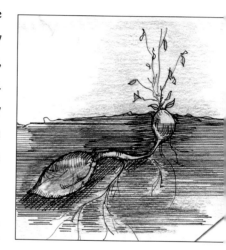

**The amazing work of seeds.
A lot goes on that we can't see.**

Egg Carton Gardens and "Egg"cellent Gifts

Egg cartons also work well. Punch holes in the bottom of each egg pouch and set the cartons in a plastic tray or baking dish. If you use a cardboard

egg carton you can plant the whole thing right in the ground when your seedlings are ready. The cardboard will decompose in time.

An "egg-cellent" way to start plant seedlings.

For a nice homemade gift to a gardener, decorate a carton with bright colors or pictures of flowers and give a dozen seedlings as a present!

Dying of thirst from too much water: Impossible? Not with plants. If the roots are watered too much they actually get soft and start to rot. Roots grow by a need to find water to support the plant. If they're soaked and surrounded with water they won't spread out. They become "lazy" and weak. Sometimes it really pays to have to work for something. When they start to rot they aren't strong enough to move the water from the soil to the plant and the plant will begin to dry out. A good rule is to let the soil almost dry out totally before watering again. If it sticks to your finger, wait a few hours.

Depending on just how much sun pours through your window you will have to water a little every few days. The good news is that you should be able to tell how the plants are doing just by looking at them. They should have strong stems and good green foliage and not be weak and bending over. They should look like you feel on a nice day—ready to go; ready for anything. Remember, it's easier for plants and soil to dry out when they're outside. Sometimes inside we give them too much of a good thing.

To keep your roots from getting too soggy, place something beneath your seed tray or pots. Bubble wrap works well. The small bubbles of air raise the pots and allow air to move through and across the bottoms. It helps keep the soil from getting soggy. Or, line the bottom of the tray with plastic wrap. On top of the plastic, place a layer of small pebbles. On top of the pebbles place your seed containers (peat pots, egg cartons, seed trays, etc.). Pet stores that sell fish tanks also sell small, clean pebbles.

Too big: If the plants get too big and it's not warm enough outside yet, you may have to place them in a larger container. You can plant them individually in a cut-down one-quart milk carton with some holes in the bottom; or place together in some kind of big shallow box. Some supermarkets have boxes that have a wax coating on them to keep them from rotting when they're wet.

Hooray for clay: Clay pots are by far the best pots for the environment. When they are done with their useful lives as pots, they can go back into the ground. Clay is really nothing more than worn-down rocks or dirt that ends up in the ground. Clay is found at the bottoms of riverbeds. This mushy stuff is dug up, formed, fired (cooked), and made into pots and other things. Many years ago, people used to make houses out of clay. Some cultures still do.

There is something special about making a pot out of dirt to hold dirt and plants: a nice part of the "cycle." And clay pots are available in all sizes from tiny to huge.

Decorating Clay Pots

You can buy fancy pots or use your creativity to decorate clay pots. Because they're made of natural clay, they have no negative environmental impact. They don't last forever but they'll look nice for years. Try acrylic paints, and paint decorations such as flowers or stripes around the rim. You'll have your own custom-made line of pots.

COLD FRAMES or "sun boxes" are another great way to

get a head start on the season. Cold frames are actually "warm" frames. These are simply boxes with glass, clear, or frosted plastic tops that in late winter or early spring you can set outside in the sun. By closing the glass top, the plants are kept warm but receive the full advantage of sunshine. You can put your trays of peat pots in a cold frame instead of on a windowsill. On warm days you can open or remove the top and let some good cool air inside the box. Close it at night. This helps the plants "harden" off. That just means we're toughening them up to get them ready to be set outside in the garden in a few weeks.

Keep the box off the ground so a big snowstorm won't bury it. The snow probably won't hurt the plants, but it might be hard to find the cold frame. Snow can help keep them warm, actually. But if they stay buried too long they'll suffer from lack of sun and light. One way to keep warmth in the box is to insulate the sides by piling up leaves or compost along the edges.

Plants that do well in cold frames are:

Broccoli

Cabbage

Lettuce

Other leaf vegetables like spinach and kale

Depending on your point of view, a cold frame is also often called a "sun box."

How to Build a Simple Cold Frame

One way to create a cold frame is to find an old window that's not being used anymore, measure it, and design the frame for it. Use lumber (cedar is best and will last a long time, but regular pine is okay too, and less expensive) that has dimensions of 1" x 8" or 1" x 10" for the sides. Build a box large enough to support your plants, but small enough to be moved. You'll need a bottom to the box; this can be either plywood or a cedar lattice panel. Then you'll need hinges to attach the window to the frame. Now you have yourself a nice "cold frame." If you don't hinge it, make sure you build handles so you can lift the cover off.

HARDENING OFF. Some plants need to be started indoors and then gradually set out to harden off (or toughen up). We can do this either by using a cold frame, as mentioned above, or simply by setting the plants out on cool days and bringing them in at night.

List of Plants That Benefit from Hardening Off

The following do wonderfully when moved to a cold frame or brought outside in their pots a couple of weeks before they're ready to be set out in the garden:

Tomatoes	**Broccoli**
Cucumbers	**Cabbage**
Peppers	**Cauliflower**

BRINGING THE OUTSIDE IN. If you

can't wait for some color before the winter finally ends, you can bring cuttings of certain plants inside. If you have a shrub called forsythia, for instance, just go out and cut a few branches off with a sharp pruner. Bring them inside, put them in a few inches of water in a container or vase, and place it in a sunny window. Wait a couple of weeks. Even

Forsythia branches blooming.

Apple blossoms have a wonderful aroma.

if there's still snow on the ground outside, you'll have beautiful yellow blooms inside.

Other plants such as flowering cherries, apples, or azaleas can be forced to bloom inside like this with very little effort. In early spring, before trees and shrubs bloom, you can look around and see if there are any branches broken from the snow. If there are buds on the branches, bring them inside. You should make a new, clean cut where the branch is broken. Ask for a pair of pruning shears. Good pruning shears are quite sharp so make sure you have an adult around to use them carefully. Put the branch in water in a sunny window and watch spring arrive early inside your house.

Once the buds open and they're in full bloom, move them out of the full sun and occasionally mist the foliage and branches with a spray bottle of water. The blooms can last for a few weeks.

When the branches are finished blooming, you can add some of these to the compost pile. The branches will recycle and the shrub or tree will grow plenty of new branches to replace the ones you cut away.

Forsythia, in bloom outside, are one of the first signs that spring has arrived and a great indication that the soil temperatures are warming, even if there's still a bit of snow on the ground or on the way. You can actually track soil temperatures by observing the flowering period of certain plants. For instance, people who take care of lawns and don't like crabgrass know that the time to treat the lawn for crabgrass prevention is between forsythia and lilac bloom.

Simple Window Gardens

If you have a sunny window and some space on the sill you can make a window garden. Find a large plastic tray (2" or 3" deep). Put some small stones on the bottom and fill it with planting soil. (Remember, avoid "wet feet." Most plants want to dry out between waterings.) Plant small decorative plants that you can buy in hardware stores called sedums, or a plant called hens and chicks.

They can survive with very little water, so only water the tray once per week. If you'd like, you can add some nice rocks to the surface and you'll have a miniature rock garden—or even a miniature desert. In spring you can plant these outside in a sunny spot of the garden. (See the section on roof gardens.)

Hens and chicks need very little water and lots of sun.

Hairy Man

The experience of watching things grow is fun and exciting. Here's a fun experiment. Buy or make some funny-looking eyes and glue them onto the side of a round peat pot. Fill the pot with planting soil and plant fast-growing annual rye grass seed. Most seed companies sell a "quick mix" that will germinate between four to seven days.

The grass will grow before your eyes—which means very quickly—in sunshine. The googly-eyed pot will look like it's growing crazy hair. It's just a fun example of how seeds grow. You can transplant this out into the lawn right in the peat pot, but the annual grass will vanish in the winter.

Small clay pots give a nice "earthy" look to a window herb garden. The herbs can be used for "spicing up" the kitchen throughout the year.

 # Mini Herb Garden

Herbs are plants we grow and use for spices in cooking, for medicines, and as tea. Many of them are fragrant, which means they smell nice. The foliage (leaves) also have nice color and texture, which make them a nice part of the "indoor landscape."

You can create a small herb garden in a sunny window in much the same manner you started other plants inside. The best way to do this is to start the herb plants or seeds in clay pots (4–6" inches in diameter) in your sunniest window. If you have a sunny kitchen window, that's the best because you can simply pick off the herbs for cooking right from your indoor garden. Herbs do like humidity (moisture in the air), so if you place the pots on a shallow tray and keep some water and stones in the bottom, they'll be more content in the house.

GROWING A VEGETABLE GARDEN

G rowing food is one of the most important reasons we have gardens. People all over the world live on the food they produce in their own garden. It is something of a miracle when we push a seed into the good ground in one season and harvest its crop in another. Whether you're a young, beginning gardener or an experienced pro, this simple truth is pretty amazing.

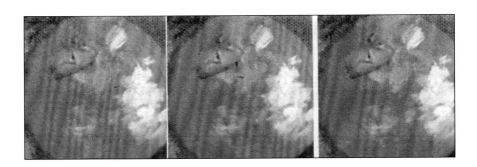

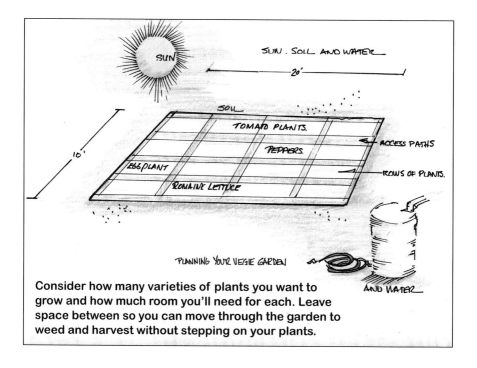

SUN . SOIL AND WATER

PLANNING YOUR VEGIE GARDEN

AND WATER

Consider how many varieties of plants you want to grow and how much room you'll need for each. Leave space between so you can move through the garden to weed and harvest without stepping on your plants.

 # Planning the Garden

It's important to think about how large a garden you want and what shape. What do you want to grow? You need a different plan for a flower garden or a vegetable garden or even a butterfly garden. You can start small if you're a beginner. A lot depends on how much space you have available. Some vegetables, such as gourds and pumpkins, need a lot of room. How much sun comes into your yard? Plants like tomatoes need a lot of sun. Make a list of what you want to plant, get a big piece of paper, and start trying to figure out where you might place each plant. Make your plan colorful and bright. It's going to be a garden after all. Some of the fun of gardening is in the imagining and anticipation.

When you plan your space, make sure you have a source of water available. Check out the "rain barrels" activity in Chapter 9. Over-crowding can also shade the soil. Leave a 15–24"-wide path between rows. Some of the vine plants (like cucumbers and pumpkins) can grow around the rows and beneath taller plants like tomatoes. Tomato plants will need to be tied to wooden stakes or grown in wire cages that you can buy at most stores.

I've seen all kinds of gardens growing successfully in all kinds of shapes and forms. So get creative and have some fun.

Spring comes in like a lion and leaves like a lamb.

A vegetable garden can be an attractive part of the landscape.

Lions and Lambs

March is an important month for gardeners. In the northeast we often say March comes in "like a lion" and leaves "like a lamb." It sort of takes us by the hand and walks us from winter into spring.

The days get longer and warmer and, despite the occasional snowstorm, we know spring is just around the corner. Once things begin to dry out and the frost is out of the ground we can start preparing the garden. Wherever you live your climate is unique. An important part of good gardening is coming to understand your own climate and seasons.

RAISED BEDS. One of the best ways to make a garden is by raising it up. This makes it easier to work and weed and helps it dry out faster between watering. Raising beds usually allows for earlier gardening because the soil warms more quickly. Another reason to create a raised bed is that you can establish better soil conditions. Top soil, compost, and manure are the perfect ingredients for any garden soil.

Building Simple Raised Beds

1. First of all, select a sunny spot. Most flowers and vegetables prefer sun.

2. Start simple: You don't always need to build a border or frame. You can simply lay old newspaper down on the existing ground and add compost and top soil on top to create a raised area of good dirt.

3. How far up should a raised bed be? Raising the bed up 8–10" inches or even more makes it easier to work around and harvest and ensures good, rock-free soil conditions.

4. Framework: If you prefer a neater, more contained look, you can pile rocks or old brick around the border to hold the soil in place. There are lots of ornamental blocks available that will do the same.

You can build raised beds out of cedar, which lasts a long time and weathers well.

5. Construction: 2" x 6" planks work well; 1" x 6" can also work but will need more bracing. You'll need to establish vertical braces to hold the frame. See the photo below of a unique solution to a cedar planter constructed by friends of mine. There are no limits to design or construction. Most are simple rectangles narrow enough to reach from all sides. Design your raised beds to fit your site. Make the raised bed a nice part of the overall landscape.

This is a raised bed my friends built in their backyard. They used two store-bought kits and combined them creatively. You can see their granddaughter, Kayla, enjoying the fruits of their labor.

PREPARING YOUR GARDEN SOIL. If it's a
new garden, and there is grass growing, you'll have to remove the grass or turn the top soil and sod (grass) over well with a shovel and rake the soil under the grass into the bed. Grass roots cling to the best top soil. Shake off the roots and use that nice soil. Adding your own compost, or prepared compost you can purchase at a local garden center, and some dehydrated (no water content) or composted manure will help create good soil for your garden. Now your dirt has become garden soil. Remember: next year, the best time to get the garden ready is in the fall. But if it's a new garden, just start when you're able.

Preparing your garden site in advance

If you plan ahead here's an easy way to get your garden started. Cut a thick clear plastic sheet to the size you would like your garden. Lay it out in a sunny spot in the yard where you would like your garden. Put some stone, boards, or bricks around the plastic to hold it down flat. Then just leave it. Whether it's lawn or weeds beneath, the clear plastic will make the sunlight more intense and burn up things beneath it. (Don't worry, the worms can scurry away to cooler spots . . . but weeds can't scurry.)

After a few weeks in full sun, the grass will be burned away and it'll be easier for you to begin to turn the ground over.

If you're preparing in the fall for next year's garden, this is a great time to start creating your own compost pile. Remember to save fall leaves and other debris from the yard and kitchen to add to your compost. And this winter you can plan the details of your new garden. (See Chapter 12 for information about composting.)

Have a rake on hand.

Turning over soil:

This can be done with elbow grease and a good shovel. Dig, turn, and chop. That's basically the work of turning over a garden. You're trying to mix up the top 6–8"-of soil and make it loose and rock free. Or, your family can rent a machine called a rototiller to make it easier to turn the top 6–8" of soil over. Or chip in with a neighbor and you can take turns using it. An adult should run the rototiller . . . but it's fun to watch it chew up the soil.

PLANTING SEEDS DIRECTLY INTO THE GROUND. Read the seed packets to see if a plant

prefers sun (most do) or shade.

Planting Seeds Directly in the Garden

As soon as the soil can be worked, you can plant:

Peas	Spinach	Pumpkins
Beans	Squash	Gourds
Lettuce	Zucchini	

You can also start these seeds indoors, but these are all hardy plants that will grow directly from seed in the garden. As an experiment, plant seeds of each inside peat pots and also directly in the garden and have a race. Which will grow fastest? Will one produce more vegetables than the other? Which method will you choose next year? Gardening is a science and an art. Experimenting is part of the science of good gardening.

How deep to plant a seed?

The seed packets always tell you the recommended depth at which the seed should be planted. Get an old-fashioned wooden ruler so you can check depths easily. And once your garden soil is ready, the ruler will help you make sure there are no hidden rocks or anything else that might get in the way of your new roots. Some seeds can be planted in rows. This means you need to dig a shallow trench and place all of the seeds in the trench. Then simply fill the trench gently and press the soil down. I find a closed fist works well for this.

 # Fancy Plant Markers

Now that you've planted some seeds, how are you going to remember what they are? One of the complicated things about a garden is once you plant the plants or seeds there is a wait—many days or sometimes weeks—before they germinate and even more before they flower or bear fruit. In

the meantime, it's easy to forget what you planted and where. You can buy plant markers that you can write on. But it's more fun to decorate your own, using popsicle sticks, wooden tongue depressors, or paint stirrers, available from paint stores. Paint stirrers are great because they're so big. You can write the name of the plant, or paint a picture of what the anticipated flower or vegetable will look like, right there on the stick. The seed packet will have a great picture. Use pencils to outline the plant and acrylic or tempura paint to color them in. If you add beautiful pictures to your markers, they become an attractive addition to the garden.

MAKING A BREAK FOR IT: MOVING YOUR INDOOR PLANTS OUTSIDE.

The plants' young roots (they probably look like tiny white hairs) might already be sticking right through the sides and bottoms of their peat pots. That's a good thing. They are ready to make a break. When gently tucked in the ground, the roots push their way right through the pot and take off into the good top soil. The bigger root system is going to support a bigger plant as it grows. Check it in a few days. You might be amazed. The pot simply breaks down and becomes part of the planting soil. If the top rim of the peat pot is sticking up over the soil level, simply tear it off so it doesn't draw moisture away from the plant.

As you move your plants off their trays and into the ground, be gentle and try not to disturb the roots. If you've already transplanted into a big box or a bigger container, you simply have to carefully pull the roots from the soil. An old spoon or a tongue depresser will work well.

Set the plant in the ground at the height of the soil in the pot and then tap the soil around it gently with your knuckles. This gets rid of air pockets. Just try to remember to wipe your knuckles off when you're done, or all that good soil is going to end up in your pockets. I speak from experience.

After planting, moisten the soil. Don't flood it; water it gently and slowly so the water can seep into the soil around the roots.

PLANTING A VEGGIE GARDEN—A MONTH-BY-MONTH GUIDE. Here's a

short list of a few easy plants. As you begin to enjoy gardening I'm sure you'll add your own favorites.

March

Lettuce (leaf lettuce) in this sense is not the usual head lettuce called iceberg. Head lettuce forms a round fold of leaves that is harvested as one. Leaf lettuce can be picked leaf by leaf and added to a salad or a sandwich as you desire through the spring and into early summer in many regions. There are many varieties of leaf lettuce plants that can grow and benefit from the long cool spring season.

Peas can be planted even if there's still snow on the ground. Plant them close together in a shallow trench, about 4" deep. And you can crowd them and let them grow thick. Find some sticks lying around the yard from the long winter and stick them in the ground among the pea seeds. The little branches will support the foliage (leaves) of the new pea plants. Pea plants grow upward and will cling and climb as they grow.

Spinach is another cool weather crop that you can set out in March. I like it in salad, but some people love it cooked. Either way, it's very good for you. Leaf crops, like leaf lettuce and spinach, prefer soil with **nitrogen**[7] (a natural chemical that some plants need to grow). If you have added good compost to your garden soil you might have plenty of nitrogen in your soil already. Spinach doesn't like hot weather and will "go to seed," which means it will start to produce flowers with seed pods, as soon as the season heats up. And when leaf crops go to seed, the leaf suffers and doesn't taste as good.

---

7   Nitrogen: a gaseous element that is a part of living tissue

April

Broccoli is a heavy "feeder." This means it should have good rich soil around its roots. You should also add **lime** (ground-up limestone) because the roots can get something called "clubroot," which will stunt the growth of the plant. Club root is a fungus. Lime is rich in calcium (a mineral that we humans need for healthy bones). Calcium kills the fungus. Lime powder is available at garden supply stores and is easy to use. It's easier if you start it indoors or purchase started plants from a garden store, because it can take a while to start working. Broccoli is one of those that benefits from hardening off a few weeks before planting.

Dill (for pickles!) is really easy to grow. It's an **herb**[8]. Make sure it's in full sun. Plant the seeds shallow, only about ¼" deep, and tamp loose soil over them. Just add water every day and the plants may get as high as three feet tall.

April would be the month you start hardening off the rest of the plants you started indoors (like tomatoes, cucumbers, eggplants, and peppers, and whatever else you still have on your windowsill). Place the plants—in their containers—outside on warm days and bring them in at night.

Cherry tomatoes are a great snack.

May

Tomatoes: Where I live in the northeast, we have to start tomatoes inside in a greenhouse or a cold frame—our warm season just isn't long enough—or buy tomato plants from

---

8   Herb: a plant or part of a plant used for flavoring, aroma, or medicinal purposes

a nursery. But if you grew your own from seeds, it's time to set them out in the garden.

If you grew them in trays or bought them from a nursery in trays, they can be gently separated and set in the ground. If you grew them in peat pots you can put the whole thing right in the ground and the plant will continue to grow without being disturbed. Bury the main stalk a few inches deep. Keep the plants about 24–36" apart.

Plant them in full sun and place a sturdy stake next to them so you can tie them up as they grow. You can make your own stakes out of sticks that are at least ¾" thick and 3' tall. And at a local garden supply store you'll find some ties that you can use that won't hurt the plants. Try a few different varieties of tomatoes. They come in red, orange, and yellow and lots of different sizes. My favorites are cherry tomatoes.

Container Tomato Garden

If you don't have enough space in the garden, or if you live in an apartment or someplace with limited yard space, you can grow tomatoes in a large container. Use a prepared soil mix and put the plant in full sun. You'll eventually need a stake to keep the plant upright unless you plant some of the new compact patio plant varieties. But you can grow any kind of tomato plant in a container. Add an herb

You don't necessarily need a big space for a nice little garden.

like oregano to the surrounding soil. The tomato plant grows tall and the oregano stays low. You can also add flowers like marigolds around the base, and you'll have your own little mini landscape. Remember to let the soil dry between watering. Soil stays moist longer in a container. This is why clay is better than plastic for a container garden. Clay allows for air exchange through its surface and excess water can evaporate more easily.

Peppers: Start the plants inside or purchase plants already started. Wait a couple of weeks after the last frost in spring and then set them in the ground in full sun, about 24" apart. They like good, rich soil and will appreciate it if you add compost and other organic stuff to your garden. A couple of pepper plants can also be grown in a container in full sun. They just need some room to trail over the pot, and you might need to stake them.

Squash: There are lots of different kinds of squash, from zucchini to spaghetti squash. You can plant these as seeds or transplant your indoor plants in slightly raised hills in the garden. Give these plenty of room (at least a foot between mounds). They can take up lots of space. Spaghetti squash actually separates like pasta noodles when cooked. Try it with homemade tomato sauce created from your own home-grown tomatoes and herbs.

Pumpkins: Pumpkins need lots of space. Dig a hole about 6" deep and a foot wide and fill it with soil. Create a mound about 5–6" tall of good rich organic soil. Then press a half dozen pumpkin seeds into the mound. You'll need about 8–10' between mounds to grow nice pump-kins. After a week you can pull the weaker seedlings from the mounds and let the remaining ones grow and thrive.

Cucumbers: Like tomatoes, you may need to start cucumber seeds inside or in a cold frame or greenhouse. Cucumbers grow on sprawling vines and ripen in summer. Try planting them by seed directly in your garden one summer and start them indoors the next. See which works best.

Activity — Something Sour: Growing and Making Pickles

Grow both your cucumbers and dill in full sun. Plant after all the frost is past. When the dill flowers, it is ready to harvest. Pick the dill and let it dry. There are lots of kits with ready-made mixes to make delicious pickles from your cucumbers.

You can make your own homemade pickles simply by soaking cucumbers overnight in vinegar and water, adding spices like garlic and dill. The longer they soak, the more sour they will become. There are lots of different recipes available and all are quite simple. Try a few until you find one you like and then make it your own with a unique twist. Give it a name like "Peter Piper Pickles" if your name happens to be Peter Piper.

June

Corn: Music to your ears? No, I don't suggest you go out and sing to your corn plants, but the truth is the corn fruit (kernels) form along something that is called an ear. And what the heck, there's no better place to sing than in a garden on a sunny day. And the ears of corn won't complain, even if you can't hold a tune.

Set the corn kernels out in mounded rows with the plants about two feet apart. Plant the seeds and remove the weaker seedlings once

Some folks claim your corn plants should be as high as an elephant's eye by the fourth of July.

they sprout. If you have room, leave at least three feet between rows. Plant at least four rows to ensure good pollination. (The bugs and the birds will help with this . . . and even the wind.) You can plant different varieties.

My favorite corn variety is "Silver Queen." Its small white kernels are delicious.

 # A Popcorn Garden

Imagine looking out your window and seeing your garden explode into popcorn. Well that's not exactly how it happens, but the truth is that a long time ago, this may have been how popcorn was discovered. Popcorn is simply a type of corn that has a little bit of moisture and starch inside the kernel. When it's exposed to heat the moisture inside expands and "pops."

You can make your own popcorn garden. The simplest way is to just buy a sack of popcorn at the grocery store. Take some of the kernels and place

Popcorn was discovered when corn "popped" in the garden.

them in a damp paper towel or cloth and keep them in a cool dark place. You'll see them begin to sprout. Once the chance of frost is gone, set a bunch of the sprouted kernels about a half-inch deep in the good top soil of your garden. Leave about two feet between seeds. The plants will grow tall, so plant them in rows you can walk between. You'll have to water them regularly so they'll grow strong and healthy.

Once the ear of corn forms and matures in summer, you can pick it from the stalk, open it up, and take the new kernels from it. Lay the harvested kernels on newspaper or paper towels and store them in a cool dry place for about fourteen days. These should be ready to heat up. The heat causes the inside of the kernel to expand and pop. Once that happens, the only popping left to do is into your mouth with the great snack you grew yourself. And you can store some kernels away for fall and winter. Put them in a jar, and store with a fun, creative label.

An Amazing Maize Maze

What's a maize maze? Well that's just a tricky way of saying "corn maze." You can create a corn maze if you have enough room to plant a lot

of corn. You'll need at least sixteen rows each way in an area about 30' x 30'. Larger is even better, but

An amazing maize maze. This one's a simple one. You can get complicated.

it depends on how much room you have in the yard. And it might be fun to just experiment with a small one.

See the layout above to create secret paths in your corn maze.

A Salsa Garden

Try growing beefsteak and Tuscany tomatoes. If you like spicy stuff, grow some hot peppers to add to your own homemade salsa. Try growing chili peppers. Just a few plants will give you plenty of hot stuff to add to your salsa. They need full sun and plenty of water.

Simple Salsa (Also Called Pico de Gallo)

The origin of the name is something of a mystery because it translates to English as "Beak of the Rooster." It may refer to the shape of a chili pepper, which might resemble a beak, or the sharp feeling on the tongue.

Pico de Gallo
Ingredients

3 or 4 plum tomatoes or any medium-sized tomato

1 white (or red) onion, medium-sized

½ cup chopped cilantro leaves

1 chili pepper, jalapeño, or cayenne (these can be from your garden or bought in the grocery store)

1 small lime

With adult supervision for younger children, use a sharp knife to carefully slice the tomatoes into ¼"-thick slices. Then cut again across the slices to "dice" the tomatoes into little ¼" squares. Put aside in a bowl and allow some of the juice to drain away.

Peel the onion. Slice and dice into cubes (about ½ the size of the tomato chunks) and put in the bowl with the diced tomatoes. (Note: Have a box of tissues nearby because slicing onions makes a lot of people's eyes tear up.)

Be careful handling the pepper because these are hot stuff. Cut the pepper into small pieces, removing the seeds and stems to discard. You can add some of the seeds if you like it hotter, but you should try it without first. Wash your hands well after handling peppers before you touch anything else, especially your eyes.

Cut the lime into quarters.

Combine all of the ingredients in a bowl. Squeeze the juice of two or three of the lime quarters into the mix.

Place in the refrigerator for about an hour.

Get some chips, start scooping, and enjoy a delicious fresh snack from the garden.

Strawberries, those delicious juicy red fruits, are 100 percent more tasty when you grow them yourself. Buy the plants from a nursery and place them a spot in your garden where they can live for years and not get dug up each spring. Most are perennial, so they come back every year, but many won't bear fruit until the second year. So it takes patience, but it is well worth the wait. And the leaves are sharp and shiny, so the plants are pretty and the flowers are nice while you're waiting. Strawberry plants are vigorous growers and re-root themselves, so leave some room to expand.

 Strawberry Pots

You can buy special pots at nurseries that have holes in the sides so the strawberry vines can spill right out. Fill the tall pots with good potting soil and

Ripe for the picking: strawberry plants spill right out of their pot.

STRAWBERRY POT

plant the roots of the plants in the top, and into the holes along the side of the pot. They'll sprout out with sun and water and the plants will spill out of the pot, create flowers, and form strawberries in July. These can be fun to watch and great to harvest. Sometimes you can buy the pot all set up with soil and plants and all you have to do is add sunshine and water. If you set these in a sunny window in early spring you'll have a head start and may even get some fruit early.

Garden Journal

Keep a log for next year indicating what does well and what doesn't.

With gardening, experience is the best teacher. The earliest gardeners must have made a lot of mistakes before they figured out the best plants for food and flower. You can do the same by keeping a record of your successes and failures.

Anyone who has gardened knows there are plenty of mistakes to make. And sometimes after the winter it's easy to forget your mistakes as well as your great ideas. So by keeping a garden journal you can keep a simple record of what happened, from growing the seeds to seeing the flowers or eating the vegetables or fruit. It's a great way to learn and become a better gardener with each year. Once again, get creative. Decorate your journal with drawings or pictures of your gardens and add some notes on how much fun you had working in the garden or eating the great homegrown food. Collect some simple recipes for all of your own creations.

WORMS AND OTHER FRIENDS

Now you know that good, healthy top soil is alive. The most important critter in most of our soil and gardens is the earthworm.

Captain Earthworm. Long and skinny and sort of the color of a rainy day and actually a little wet and soggy like that too, the earthworm just may be the captain of the **ecological**[9] ship out in your yard. If they could, I'm sure they'd have a whistle like a coach or a gym teacher, but earthworms do their work silently.

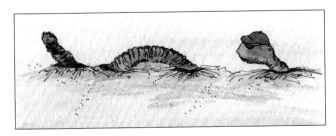

---

9 Ecological: a part of science that studies organisms and their natural environment

Most of their good work is underground. They like things cool and moist. That's why you'll occasionally see them lying around on the surface on rainy and overcast days, looking kind of lazy.

But their work is *so* important.

Boiled Spaghetti. Pick up a handful of cooled cooked spaghetti (I recommend doing this before the sauce is applied) and feel it slide between your fingers.

Feels funny, right? It's the closest way to imagine exactly what an earthworm feels like.

It's the earthworms' slimy skin that allows them to slither through soil and leave tiny tunnels behind them. These tunnels allow air and water to move freely through the soil to help the roots of the plants in your garden. Even the warmth of the spring sun can be drawn through these tunnels to warm the roots of plants. They crawl their way through the harder ground (called **hardpan**[10]) and in between all the rocks that haven't rolled quite enough. And they've been doing this for millions of years.

Eating Machines

As if this isn't enough, earthworms do even more. They're eating machines. These critters are constantly eating as they move. They

---

10 Hardpan: a compacted hard layer of soil

Worms like it cool and moist.

sort of eat their way forward. Their favorite foods are in the soil around them. Earthworms especially love things like **fungus**[11] and **algae**[12] and even **bacteria**[13].

The greatest thing about worms is that they take all this stuff they eat and process it through their wiggly, slimy bodies and turn it into food for the soil and things that grow. What comes out of the worms is lunch for our soil and plants. Moving through this dark and wet world they leave behind what are called castings—the digested plant food. The big, long name for this is **vermipost**. "Worm poop" works too.

So next time you see a worm on the cool ground you might want to say thanks.

Worm Bin

There are lots of worm bins available at stores. But you can make your own by using plastic bins. Don't use clear bins because the sun will heat up the interior and, remember, worms prefer cool. Start with a couple of plastic bins with five to ten holes punched or drilled through the bottom of one. Place the one with holes on top of the other and connect them with wire or clips. Make small holes in the cover of the top bin.

---

11 Fungus: a type of plant that includes mushrooms and mildews

12 Algae: tiny plants that thrive in moist conditions

13 Bacteria: very tiny plants that live in soil and water and can be beneficial to people

A worm "high rise"

Fill the top one with compost material like peat moss, coffee grounds, tea bags, and even shredded newspaper. The worms will feed on this stuff and create that great natural fertilizer vermipost. The rich vermipost will settle through the holes and the bottom bin will fill with great stuff for your garden.

Place the bins in the shade of the yard. If you want to do this in the winter they'll need to be kept inside or moved to a place that doesn't freeze.

You can add a third bin on top of the second and more worms after you've had some success. And when your garden looks better than ever remember to tip your cap your wiggly friends.

A Few Other Good Bugs

The Ladies of the Landscape: Ladybugs (Lady Beetles)

These are those pretty red bugs that you see out in the yard and let crawl on your finger. But don't be surprised if they suddenly take off and fly away. Ladybugs can only fly in warm weather and can go a long distance south as winter approaches.

Ladybugs are good for the yard because they eat bugs that are not good for plants, like aphids, scale (which are another type of very small flying insect), and mites. The same thing that might attract us to ladybugs—their bright colors—are just the thing that helps protect the ladybugs from other insects and predators (such as insect-eating birds) that might not want to treat them like a lady. Birds and other insects shy away from the bright colors.

Painting Ladybug Rocks

Find a smooth round stone at least as big as your fist. Wash and clean it and let it dry. Find a good picture of a ladybug with the bright red shell and the black polka dots and draw it with pencil or chalk on the stone. Then paint the stone just like a ladybug. It makes a great paperweight or a door-stop or just something to keep on your desk or shelf or even in the garden.

Bugs that Pray.

Praying Mantis. Well, they're not exactly praying. They get their name from their big front legs that are bent and held together as they stand. To some, they look they're praying. They're usually green or brown in color and they can grow up to 6" long. They have huge appetites and eat flies, moths, mosquitoes, and even cockroaches.

Praying Mantis

Lacewings (or Flying Lions) are actually called "aphid lions." That's because they hunt and then eat a lot of aphids, spider mites, white flies, mealy bugs, and others that are *not* good for our gardens.

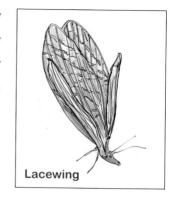

Lacewing

Dragonflies. These beautiful insects have been around for over three hundred million years and archeologists have found fossil imprints that show that in the time of the dinosaurs, these bugs were over two feet long. The good thing about them now is that they eat pesky bugs like gnats, mayflies, and mosquitoes.

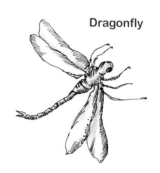

Dragonfly

Bees. One of the best bugs to see in the backyard, the honeybee, is a valuable pollinator. Pollination is when the pollen of one flower is transferred to another flower and fertilizes the new plant.

Like a little delivery service, the honeybee pollinates almost 10 percent of the world's food crops. And lately there has been a drop

Bee

in bee population and activity. That's not so good and there are many people working to keep the bee population healthy.

Other bees and wasps do some of the same but are nowhere near as good or busy as the honeybee. But the other bees and wasps feed on rotten fruit and harmful caterpillars, so they're helpful too. Just don't mess with them in the yard, because they have a pretty mean sting when they're disturbed. All bees give us a lot more good than bad.

Butterflies. Butterflies are so cool, I've given them their own chapter called Flying Flowers (see Chapter 7).

A HEALTHY MIX. In the long run, a good mix is the healthiest thing for the garden and landscape. This means insects and birds and rain and lots of different types of plants. This is called bio-diversity. But all it really means is allowing everything into the celebration we call nature. It helps keep the circle rolling like a wheel.

Some insects *can* be a nuisance and some insects can harm your favorite plants. But most insects are really good for us and very important, so we should be careful of what we spray or treat them with.

Part Two:

Summer

5

FUN WITH FLOWERS

Flowers paint the landscape with beautiful color and draw many people to the art of gardening. In fact some of the reasons many flowers are bright and beautiful is to attract insects and birds for the purpose of pollination and survival. As beautiful as they often are, flowers are really the part of the plant that forms to produce fruit and seeds.

Some flowers, called **perennials**, come back every year—usually bigger and stronger. Other flowers bloom all summer but die with the cold winter. These are called **annuals**. There's a place in every garden for both kinds of flowers. Some of these annuals will leave seeds and a new generation of annual flowers will come up in their place on their own.

If you're going to start a flower garden, choose a spot and figure out about how much sunshine you get in that spot. This will help you determine what flowers to plant. There are plants for all types of locations. Some like sun, and some like shade. Most like a little watering. But they all give back a lot more than they require.

Here are a few simple perennial plants for sun and shade—in ABC fashion. There are thousands of them.

FOR SUN

Asters : a daisy-like flower that blooms in summer and fall. The flowers are pink, purple, red, white, and lots of shades in between.

Asters

Bellis

Coreposis

Bellis: an English Daisy, mixed white, pink and red in midsummer.

Coreposis: a yellow flowering shrubby perennial that blooms from summer into fall.

FOR SHADE

Astilbe: comes in white, pink, red, and all shades in between. It has a fern-like leaf and a feathery flower in June.

Brunnera: a beautiful leaf that often has speckles or stripes and supports a delicate flower of different colors.

Cimifuga: a bold foliage plant with a nice flower in pastel shades from pink to gold.

Astilbe

Brunnera

Cimifuga

Balloon Flower

Here are a few fun flowers with funny names. See if there's one just right for you. These are all perennials and will come back year after year.

Baby Sister Iris: a Siberian Iris with sky blue flowers in full sun (14" ht.). Blooms in late spring.

Ballerina Red Armeria: also called Sea Pinks (10–12" ht.). Full sun, blooms in late spring, summer.

Balloon Flower (Platycodon): they don't really grow balloons but the flower sure looks like it right before it opens. These form little air-filled blossoms before they open. And then they provide beautiful flower, in blues or pinks. Plant in sun (15–18" ht.). Blooms in summer.

Choo Choo Train Hosta: a small shade-loving plant with beautiful curly gold leaves (12" ht.).

Balloon Bud

Foliage remains beautiful from late spring into fall.

Crazy Dazy (Leucanthemum): a tall white flower with a funny name that is all white (24–30" ht.). Full sun, blooms in late summer.

Fairytale Veronica: pink flower on silver-green foliage (16" ht.). Full or partial sun, blooms in mid-summer.

Caramel Coral Bells: foliage plant, with golden colored leaves (10–12" ht.). Shade tolerant. Foliage lasts from frost to frost.

Caramel Coral Bells

Once you've planted your garden, the plants are dependent on you and your family to make sure they're watered enough and are growing well. Once in a while, pull some of the weeds around the base and pick off any brown foliage. But for the most part, these plants will do well on their own.

A GARDEN FOR GIANTS

Sunflowers: Some varieties of sunflower grow to six feet tall or more. The largest varieties are called mammoth, which means really big. They're huge. Some of the flowers are the size of a dinner plate or a Frisbee. They're usually yellow and sometimes orange—the colors of the sun—with a big brown center.

Sunflowers are easy to grow. Plant the seeds in some good top soil after all frost is gone. Water them daily and stand back. You'll be thrilled to watch how fast they do grow—especially the giant ones. Just follow the simple instructions on the seed package.

Planting a Sunflower Maze

Because these plants can grow to a towering height, people often plant them to create a maze. A maze is a path you follow—one in which you can't always see where you're going. It can be fun, especially when you're surrounded by plants and when you look up all you see are beautiful flowers. You need room for a big maze, but if you have an area of about 15' x 15' you can try one. Find a flat area of the yard that gets plenty of sun. See the corn maze for layout ideas. (page 42) Use the tall sunflowers so you can't see over them and you'll be "lost and found" in flowers.

More Snacks from the Garden

Here's another cool, healthy snack. It's actually a seed like the popcorn kernel. The sunflower seed comes in a little protective shell called a "hull," which looks a little like a swollen watermelon pit. You can break the shell away and eat the kernel inside. It's a very tasty and healthy snack.

People all over the world use sunflower seeds as a snack or a healthy ingredient in food. Sunflower oil is made by grinding up the seeds. They're heated up and strained into liquid (oil) that's used in a lot of healthy recipes and other products.

Keep a Sunflower Journal

"Putting the pedal to the metal." That's an old saying about driving a car too fast. But in this case we're talking about a flower petal. Wow, these are some fast flowers.

Sometimes parents track the growth of their kids with a pencil mark on a doorway. Well, if you do this with your sunflower, you can measure how much it grows in a day. And I'm sure you'll be surprised. Sunflowers are really in a hurry to grow up. And they do grow fast. Keep a measurement diary and take pictures. It will be fun to look at next winter when it's cold and your garden is buried in ice and snow.

 # Making Pressed Flowers—Preserving Some of Your Summer

If you would like, you can keep some flowers by drying and pressing them. This is done by cutting the fresh flowers off their stalks and placing them gently between two sheets of wax paper. Place a heavy book, such as a dictionary, on the wax paper and keep in a warm, dry place. After a week or so you can remove the book, take the flower, place it between some kind of clear paper or plastic, and tape it to a page in your journal or glue it to a board and frame it.

A garden shoe becomes a shoe garden. When you're all done with your summer garden shoes, or you've been so busy you just wore them out, you can turn them into gardens as well.

6

WEEDS AND OTHER WONDERS

One kid's weed is another kid's wonder. Ever hear that saying? Neither have I, but it sounds good, doesn't it? And this is what it means: It means that what we think of as a weed, somewhere else, someone else might consider a priceless gem in the garden. Weeds can sometimes seem like a nuisance, but they serve many purposes. Some of the bugs and caterpillars love to eat weeds, and the more varieties, the better. For instance, beautiful Monarch butterflies feed only on milkweed. All growing plants act as erosion control, weeds included. **Erosion** is when good top soil is washed away by rain or flooding. If there's nothing growing, soil—like that dirt that gets behind your ears—can be washed away pretty easily. Vegetation (leaves and stems) protects the soil from above (by keeping it cool and shaded) while the roots knit the soil in place with a firm grip below.

Some Very Friendly Weeds

Dandelions

Hunting Lions in the Lawn

One of the more common plants that grow throughout a lawn in spring and summer is the dandelion. The name dandelion comes from the French *dent-de-lion*, translated Lion's Tooth. The leaves look like long, sharp teeth and this is where they get their name.

Many people consider dandelions pesky weeds in the lawn. But the truth is, just as many people think they're great to eat. So go out in spring and summer and be a lion hunter in the yard. They taste better in spring, before they flower. And that's when you'll need to truly be a hunter, because you'll have to carefully identify the plants by their long-toothed leaves. And once they bloom, it's hard for them to hide because they have a bright yellow flower that pops up all over the lawn. The leaves taste like chicory or endive, but the whole plant is edible. You can also use the yellow part of the flower for salad. The deep taproot tastes like a cooked carrot or potato.

Some people like them steamed. There are lots of recipes available. Here's a recipe for an easy salad.

There may be lions in the lawn.

Dandelion Salad

Simply add the leaves of the dandelions—washed very well—into a regular garden salad. You can even throw a few of the washed yellow flowers in the salad. It's nutritious and tasty.

Lion's Tooth

Steamed Lion's Teeth

2 large bunches of dandelion greens, trimmed and washed well

2 tsp (10 ml) olive oil

1 cup (60 ml) low-sodium chicken or beef broth

1 tbs (15 ml) fresh basil, chopped

salt & pepper

Cut off the flowers and thick stems near the bottom. Wash the leaves and remaining stems. Chop all into small pieces.

In a large sauce pan, heat some olive oil (about a tablespoon) and place the chopped greens in it once the oil is heated. Add a tablespoon of chopped basil. Add a cup of chicken broth.

Cook for ten minutes.

Salt and pepper to taste.

Clover

White Clover: Clover is a plant that a lot of people try to get rid of in the lawn. But there are many people who actually grow clover lawns. Clover forms thick patches that don't need mowing or fertilizing, and they are very rugged and drought-resistant. They are called a nitrogen-fixing plant because they are able to get nitrogen from the air and then deposit it in the soil, which is good for other plants. They also flower and attract bees. And we know how good bees are for the garden and landscape.

The Magical Mystery of Milkweed

The plant group we call milkweed actually contains about one hundred different species. Some are perennial, others annual. Remember, perennial means they come back every year . . . like an old friend. These are some of the most important plants in nature because a lot of different critters love them for a lot of reasons. Milkweed is the meal of choice of many caterpillars. It also attracts humming-birds and honeybees.

Milkweed seeds float on silky strands.

But perhaps the most amazing relationship between plant and critter is the Monarch and the milkweed. The Monarch butterflies love the nectar of the flower and lay their eggs in the leaves. See Chapter, Flying Flowers, to learn more about attracting butterflies to the garden and the journey of the Monarch.

FUZZY PLANTS AND OTHER WEIRD STUFF. Can fuzzy plants help save the planet?

If you look closely, some plants have a light hairy texture to their surface, which protects their leaves (foliage). This is called **pubescence**. The plants are protected because the tiny hairs reflect the sunlight back and keep the plant—and the surrounding ground—cooler. Scientists have shown that when planted in mass, fuzzy plants can cool ground temperature and compete with what seems to be our warming planet.

All plants help the atmosphere because they use carbon dioxide and give off oxygen. Fuzzy plants just may have an added bonus when they reflect direct sunlight and help Earth cool down.

Here's a list of fuzzy perennial plants you can add to your garden. Most are available at garden centers:

Golden Yarrow   Lambs Ear

Silver Mound or Silver King   Silver Carpet

Prickly Pear (use for jam)   Lavender Cotton

Irish Moss   Woolly Thyme

Note: Fuzzy isn't always cute. Mature poison ivy has a hairy stem structure. This is invasive and poisonous to some people, so avoid it at all costs.

Golden Yarrow   Silver Mound   Prickly Pear

Lambs Ear

Lavender Cotton

Irish Moss

"FLYING FLOWERS": BUTTERFLIES AND BUTTERFLY GARDENS

There are over twenty thousand different kinds of butterflies, and many of them are colored so beautifully they can look like flowers in flight. And most of these beautiful creatures live only one month. Some smaller species live only one week. But in their short lives they add great beauty to the landscape and garden.

Look up as they fly through the sunlight. Sometimes the sunlight shines right though the wings like a stained-glass window.

And this is important: *Butterflies love the sunlight*, so any garden in which you plan to attract butterflies should be in a sunny location. The west or south side of your property is best.

Besides being a beautiful part of our world, butterflies are important because they pollinate plants, then in turn become a part of the **food chain**[14] as food for birds. In turn, birds help spread plant seeds. It's all part of the big cycle of life turning and rolling along.

---

14 Food chain: a sequence of living things using the "lesser" organism to feed on

BEAUTY AND THE BEAST. The change

from caterpillar to butterfly is sort of a beauty and the beast transformation. Well, not really, because a lot of caterpillars are pretty and some are even kind of cute. Some have stripes and dots. Some look exactly like the leaves they like to land and feed on. Some have colored manes and what looks like hair.

But all caterpillars become butterflies or moths. They become enclosed in something called a **pupa**[15] and, when that opens, a butterfly flies out and up toward the sun. Consider them one of nature's great gifts and invite them into your yard.

Another Shout-out to Weeds.

Many of the weeds we try to get rid of in the yard are favorite plants of caterpillars. A great yard for butterflies and caterpillars has a diverse combination of plants, including some wild or native plants we may consider weeds.

PLANTING A BUTTERFLY GARDEN.

Besides sunshine, butterflies are attracted to color. It's a good idea to plant groups of single colors: purple, red, or yellow. Plant different varieties so something is in bloom at all times.

What we call a butterfly garden is simply a garden that is planted with the idea

Butterflies feed on the nectar of the flowers. Nectar is a sugary liquid the flower produces to attract insects like butterflies and birds that will help pollinate the plant.

---

15 Pupa: a stage of a changing insect as it matures

of attracting butterflies so we can enjoy their beauty in the yard or land-scape as well as taking part in nature's circle. The gardens themselves can be beautiful but they're made even more charming with the addition of these "flying flowers."

There are lots of different kinds of butterflies and you can read about them in special books on butterflies. As an introduction I'll simply list some plants that attract varied species of butterflies.

Plants that Attract Butterflies

Agastache	Joe Pye Weed
Milkweed	Sweet William
Asters	Bee Balm
Butterfly Bush	Black-eyed Susan
Cone Flowers	Tulip Trees

Milkweed

Agastache

Asters

Butterfly Bush

Cone Flowers

Joe Pye weed

Bee Balm

Black-eyed
Susan

Activity Creating a Butterfly Garden

Find a small area you can dedicate to some of the plants that attract butterflies. Depending on how large an area you have, select some combination of plants from the list and plant them together. The best place is a sunny spot that you can see from a window but is easy to spot from the air. Bright colors attract butterflies. There are both annual and perennial plants that attract specific butterflies. Butterflies lay eggs on what are called "host plants." You can find specific varieties at local garden centers.

Include some greens like dill or parsley for the caterpillars to eat. And remember: Don't do too good a job in the fall cleaning up your garden. There may be eggs or larvae under leaves and old plants that will winter over for next year.

Once you've discovered the fun of watching butterflies come to your garden, there's a world of information available about specific plant, caterpillars, and butterflies available to you in the local library or garden center.

 ## Caterpillar Bowls

You can collect caterpillars and place them in a glass bowl or jar with a cover. Make sure there are air holes through the cover. Place a host plant or healthy leaves from a host plant and some pencil-thin sticks in the container. The host plant is the one you found the caterpillar on. Caterpillars don't need water because they get all the moisture they need from leaves. You can watch the shell form around the caterpillar (it's called a **chrysalis**) and eventually watch the butterfly emerge.

It'll be fun to watch the butterfly spread its wings and fly away. It might just head for your garden.

Caterpillar Condo:
short-term care

MONARCH BUTTERFLIES. Monarch butterflies can live up to nine months. They are unique in that they will only lay their eggs on milkweed plants. Their population is dwindling because more and more fields with milkweed get turned into housing developments, roads, or shopping malls. So if you think about it, if

there is no milkweed then there are no eggs and then no Monarch butterflies. The circle would be broken. Well, fortunately the Monarch has a lot of fans all over the world who follow in amazement the Monarch's adventure.

Their Incredible Journey North

In the cold winter months in North America, the Monarch butterflies journey to the hills of Mexico to roost. They migrate almost magically to the same places every year. They return as spring come to North America. You can track their journey though an organization known as Journey North (check out their website: http://www.learner.org/jnorth/monarch/). They have lots of activities and learning experiences for kids of all ages . . . and that includes many of us adults.

Planting Milkweed for Monarchs

Milkweed seeds should be planted inside in early spring. Buy the perennial varieties. Try using peat pots, plastic trays, or egg cartons. Plant them in the garden in late spring when the chance of frost is gone. There are lots of varieties. Choose some that are native to your area.

Butterfly Journals

The best way to learn is to take notes about what you see. Try taking some photos or drawing pictures of the different butterflies. Note the first day you see Monarchs, and you'll notice next year that they return at the same time every year. You can even cut, fold, and paste colored paper so a few of your pages open up into the forms of butterflies. The pages become wings.

Get creative with
your journal.

8

GARDENING IS FOR THE BIRDS

There's something about the quiet of birds as they fly overhead, isn't there? They can land and balance on the thinnest branch without breaking it, while they check out what's going on around them. And if you're quiet too, they might just hang around for a while.

And in the morning in spring and summer they are the first sound you hear, even before the sun rises. This is probably because from up high they can see and sense the sunrise before we can, and they chirp and sing at its arrival every morning.

Birds are a key part of the ecosystem. Besides being beautiful creatures that are fun to watch, they help pollinate flowers, spread plant seeds, and eat biting insects like mosquitoes and gnats.

Look at the amazing architecture of
this abandoned Blue Jay nest.

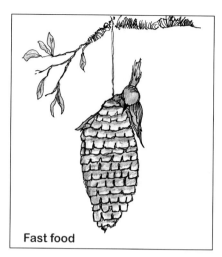

Fast food

We can encourage birds to call our yard "home" by attracting them
with flowers and food.

 How to Make Two Simple
Bird Feeders

1. Fast Food

One simple way is to roll a pinecone in peanut
butter and hang it from a tree branch. Of course,
you'll have to do this regularly. It's good, but it
doesn't last. Sort of like a fast-food meal.

2. Community Cafe.

You can take a plastic bottle (like one for soda
or juice), poke holes along the sides of it straight
though to the other side, push some thin sticks

Community Cafe

through the lower holes, and leave upper holes open for feeding. Fill it with birdseed and hang it from a tree branch. The birds will rest on the sticks and feed from the holes.

Birds can be messy, so plan on putting bird feeders where you won't mind a mess of seed casings. Their beauty can be well worth it.

Do It with Suet

For wilder birds particularly in the winter. Many stores sell suet cakes and small wire racks to hang them up in. This is an easy and reliable way to feed suet because it can be very messy to make your own. Suet is a combination of fat and meat byproducts that many wild birds love. You'll be surprised at the variety of birds that show up.

How to Build a Simple Birdhouse

Use 1" x 8" pine or cedar boards. Cedar will last longer outside and doesn't need to be stained or painted. You can make this simple birdhouse with one 8'-long board. Measure out the height you would like (15" for the back and 12" for the front works well). The width would be 7.5", which is the true width of 8" lumber. You'll need some help cutting as few angles and perhaps drilling or jig-sawing the hole. A 30-degree angle works well to slant the roof. After cutting, sand the edges with

Simple birdhouse

83

medium sandpaper. Once you've got your pieces you can glue it together with carpenter's wood glue. Most craft stores have ¼" dowels (round sticks of wood) that you can use for the perch. You'll have to drill a small hole, the diameter of the dowel, for this as well.

If you would like you can paint it or put some bird or flower decals on it. Or paint some lines that look like tree branches. Have fun with it.

Screw a hook into the balanced center of the roof. Then find an inviting place to hang it and see who moves in. If you hang it with a thin gauge wire, use a piece of rubber or plastic tubing where it warps around a branch to make sure you don't damage the bark.

PLANT FOR THE BIRDS. Birds seem to be attracted to bright colors. Many of the plants that attract butterflies also attract birds. To plan a garden that attracts birds start with a few shrubs—these are also good for birds to nest in.

Plants that Attract Birds

Astilbe	Larkspur
Butterfly Bush	Sage
Dogwood	Wine and Roses
Evening Primrose	Queen Anne's Lace
Ornamental Grass	Bee Balm
Hollyhocks	Catmint

Astilbe

Butterfly Bush

Kousa Dogwood

Ornamental Grass

Hollyhocks

Larkspur

Sage

Catmint

Wine and Roses

Bee Balm

Also plan where you might want the garden. Do you want to be able to see it from the window? Which window? Kitchen? Your own bedroom?

OTHER WAYS TO ATTRACT BIRDS TO YOUR GARDEN. Beyond plantings, here are some other ways to provide for your feathered friends.

Leave Your Leaves

Birds need to forage for food and a good source are the leaves that drop in the fall season. As much as we love to clean this up and have a neat lawn, it's much better for the birds to allow some leaves and sticks to remain as a food source through the winter. And in fact, the lawn will be fine when you clean up in spring.

Leave some leaves for the birds.

Water Features

Water attracts birds as well. Even a small birdbath is helpful in attracting birds to the yard. Just remember to keep some water in it. Birds are attracted to the sound and motion of water in a pond or stream. There are many simple waterfall systems available in garden and hardware stores. Even the simplest ones add sound and motion to the garden though simply recycling water.

This is a birdbath chiseled out of stone.

Few things are more red than a cardinal.

 # Bird Journals

Keeping a record of things in the garden is the best way to learn. Take pictures of birds and keep track of their habits. When do they come and when do they leave? What time of day? What do they seem to like the best to eat? Which plants attract them the most? The more we understand, the more we enjoy the world around us.

Try drawing or painting pictures of the birds you get to know in your yard. The colors of all the different birds can be really something. There are few things more red than a cardinal or more blue than a blue jay. Collect stray feathers in the yard and tape them in your journal.

WATER, WATER EVERYWHERE

Life couldn't exist without clean water. We're talking about liquid water, not ice and steam, or even clouds and fog.

In fact, most of Earth's surface is covered with water. But the more the human population increases, the number of machines and factories and houses increase as well, and the more impact we have on all our water. We can't solve this problem ourselves. But we can help in our own ways. Here are a few simple ways we can help in our own yards.

"A journey of a thousand miles must begin with a single step." A Chinese philosopher said that a long time ago. I don't know where he was heading, but here are a few first steps you can take.

Rain Chasers: save water one barrel at a time.

Rain barrels

GRAY WATER.

Gray water is water we collect from rain washing off the roof, and from laundry or shower water. That doesn't sound great, does it? But really it is. It's not good for drinking or cooking with, but you can use it for many other things, like watering the garden or lawn. You know those worms love the moisture.

You have heard that nice sound of rain falling on your roof in spring. Sometimes it sounds like gentle drumming. Well, that great sound means that nature is getting water and the plant roots are drinking it up. But a lot of the water that falls on the roof just gets lost in the ground around the house and doesn't help your garden much. A rain barrel is a place to catch and gather that gray water and store it so we can use it for good stuff like watering gardens or lawns during dry periods.

So to try to be a "rain chaser," ask your child if he or she would like to try catching some rain. All it really takes is a large barrel connected to a gutter downspout.

Setting Up a Rain Barrel

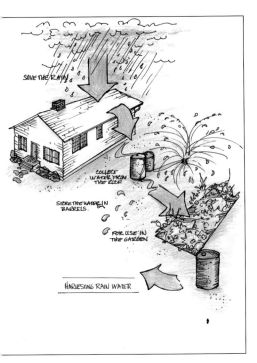

SAVE THE RAIN

COLLECT WATER FROM THE ROOF

STORE THE WATER IN BARRELS

FOR USE IN THE GARDEN

HARVESTING RAIN WATER

A rain barrel is simply a storage tank for water to use in the garden. It collects the water that falls on your roof and would ordinarily just run off the property. This stored water can easily be used to water your garden, and you'll become a part of the solution to the problem of wasted water and runoff. This is often called "harvesting rainwater." It's amazing how much water simply gets wasted. For instance, even on a small 10' x 12' shed roof, if you get an inch of rain per week, you would save 75 gallons in seven days. That's enough to water your gardens if it doesn't rain for a while.

Here's How to Harvest Gray Water

Because they are growing in popularity there are many completed rain barrels available at local garden centers and box stores as well as companies that specialize in them. They are all relatively simple and some are quite decorative. Simply, the barrel is connected on the top to a gutter downspout from a roof of the house, garage, or a shed. The gutter downspout is directed to the barrel with a plastic connecting pipe (a "downspout diverter") to an opening in the top of the barrel. Some kind of screen is needed and provided to keep debris from the water. There is a spout at the bottom to access the water with a hose connection as well as an overflow valve on top. Some of these have become pretty sophisticated, and some are made to be an attractive addition to the garden. Some actually have a well on top that can be turned into a planter in the spring and summer.

If you would like to try to make your own you'll need to find a source of a large plastic storage tank that will hold 40–60 gallons of water. If you want to experiment, start a little smaller and you may be able to make your own little system out of a large plastic water cooler and some smaller hose or tubing you can find at a hardware store. Put some kind of mesh or screening on top and a connecting pipe to your gutter downspout. Once you see how well it works, you'll probably want to move up to a larger one.

Rain Chain

A necklace for your roof? Here is a fun way to add some beauty to the landscape while using the rain to create some art and solve a problem.

One of the wonderful things about water is that it clings to surfaces as it moves downward. You've felt it drip down your cheek, haven't you? A rain chain simply offers a surface for the water to follow and creates a type of moving water sculpture when it's raining. Because it clings, it can direct the water from the roof the same way a downspout would. But a rain chain can be quite pretty. Old Japanese temples used rain chains as ornaments. In the winter, they can help create really cool icicles that look like twisted pretzels. It also helps to slow down the flowing water and disperse it instead of it just pouring out to the ground off the roof or out of a downspout. This will help prevent erosion.

You can create a rain chain by removing the downspout from your gutters at the corner of a roof line; hopefully somewhere you can see it easily from the yard and garden.

You can purchase beautiful, hand-crafted rain chains, but you can also make a simple one yourself. Cut the top inch or so off clear plastic water bottles with good scissors. You'll find they cut easily, especially if you cut along one of the existing bubble lines of the bottle. Leave the cap on and puncture a small hole in the cap. Push a thin wire (wreath-decorating wire or floral wire works well) through the hole and either tie a knot or wind a small stick or toothpick in the wire on the outside of the cap to keep the "cup" from sliding down. Measure down 3–5" on your wire and repeat until you have a chain of cups. You can do five or six or go all the way down from roof to ground. When you've pulled the wire through the last

(and highest) one, leave enough to attach to a downspout area of your roof.

When it rains, the water will follow the wire into the cup, and as each cup fills, it spills into the one below.

If it freezes in winter, you'll have a beautiful ice sculpture.

You'll be amazed how pretty the water looks as it follows the path down the chain to the ground. Especially when the sun comes back out and shines right through it.

LIVING ROOFS? EXCUSE ME, DID YOU KNOW YOUR ROOF IS ALIVE? What are living roofs? They're also called "green roofs." It might sound silly, but it's actually a really cool idea.

Green roofs mean that the whole roof or part of the roof is covered with soil and plants. This protects the home or structure from really hot temperatures as well as really cold. Many cities all over the world are starting to install green roofs on flat-topped buildings. If you have a lot of green roofs, it actually helps cool the air temperature of a city that has lots of cars and lots of people. And it absorbs some of the rain runoff just like a rain garden.

Flat roofs are best for roof gardens and that's why there are many growing in cities. The flat surface is covered with shallow trays and plants that will take the heat. Don't you think schools would be a great place to start? Lots of schools have flat roofs.

Activity!

Making Your Own Green Roof

Start small: Try building a simple shallow box (4–6" in height) or find a shallow fruit or vegetable crate. Line it with plastic. Punch holes in the bottom. Sometimes you can get low plant trays at the garden center.

Fill with a very light potting mixture. Pick out a spot on the roof that is less slanted than others and faces the sun. Porch roofs, garage roofs, and even doghouse roofs are good places to start. Purchase a variety of sedum plants at a local garden center. They require very little water. They come in burgundy and yellow and all colors in between. Plant them in the soil, water them and carefully place the planter on the roof.

Watch what the plants do from a window or the yard, and you'll begin to understand the concept of green roofs. Imagine the whole roof covered in green plants.

Some stores sell what they call "mud flats" or "coco mats." Mud flats are flat mats that have plant seeds embedded in them. Try placing these mats on a roof and see what happens.

Hens and chicks on the roof? A plant called hens and chicks is another plant that does great on the roof.

STEPPING STONES, ROCK GARDENING, AND OTHER OUTDOOR ART

STEPPING STONES—FOSSIL FORMS AND FUN WITH FUZZY FEATURES LIKE FEATHERS AND FERNS.

A fossil is an indentation or an image on an old stone that is the outline and impression of something that came to rest there and stayed for a long time as stone continued to form around it. It could be something living that died there, like a flower or an animal or an insect; or just a stick, a stone, or a shell.

Ferns can make quite an impression.

Fossils are records of the world's living past and are always exciting to discover.

Here's a way you can make your own fossil forms and create stepping stones and decorations for your gardens at the same time.

Stepping stones can be of any size and style. They can be made of concrete or plaster. The fossil impressions can be anything you'd like: pinecones, sticks, flowers, stones, or your own hand imprint. With a fossil impression, all you see is the texture (the pattern of the outside) of a thing. Pine cones leave an interesting image. There are seeds and berries and even hairy fruits or peach pits that can be used to decorate your stone. Try using those cast-off sunflower seed shells to add some texture.

Sponges have interesting textures that you can press into the surface of the plaster or concrete as it dries.

Feathers make beautifully delicate images when pressed into your plaster or concrete. If you've been encouraging the visits of birds, you'll find a few feathers in the garden that you can add as well.

Jeweled Garden Stone

Embed shiny stones in the plaster. Use these to make a design or spell words.

Plaster Collage

You can leave stones, marbles, and sticks right in the form, and you'll have a work of art or a really interesting stepping stone.

How to Make Your Stepping Stone

Plaster Stepping Stones

1. Creating the mold. Use a small pizza box, or save a heart-shaped candy box from Valentine's Day. Or save a cereal box . . . when all the cereal is gone (small boxes are best). Line the bottom of the box with wax paper or aluminum foil. Or you can make any shapes you want out of cardboard strips 2–3" wide. You'll need to set them on wax paper or foil

Sticks and stones can find a home.

before you pour your plaster. These boxes will be used to form the shape of the stone.

2. Pouring the plaster. You can either buy dry plaster of paris that you mix with water or you can make your own with white glue and water, flour, and strips of paper. Add food coloring or tempera paint to color the plaster. When the mixture is ready, simply pour it into your form.

3. Creating fossils and decorations. Give the plaster a little while to begin to set or harden, and then you can begin to "fossilize" by pressing your stones or marbles or feathers or even your own handprint into the surface of the plaster. Do it gently and hold it just long enough to make an impression in the plaster. Or you can leave the objects in place (unless it's your hand) to become a part of your stone. When you're done, let it dry overnight. The next morning, you should be able to pull the cardboard away and be left with your own fossilized garden stone.

4. Making circular stones. You can create simple circles by pouring the plaster into an aluminum pie plate. Circles make nice yellow suns or moons or flowers.

How to Make Plaster of Paris

Warm water (about 2 cups)

3 cups all-purpose flour

2 tablespoons white glue

1" strips of newspaper

Tempera paint or food coloring (optional)

Large bowl and a wooden spoon or a wire whisk to mix well.

1. Put all of the flour into a bowl and whisk it so it's not lumpy. Add the water as you stir. Add the paper slowly and continue to mix. Add the glue.

2. Keep mixing as you add food coloring or tempura paint.

3. Pour slowly into your form.

Stone Wreath

To make a plaster wreath you will need to find a mold. An aluminum pie plate with a cup in the center works. Hold the center cup down as you pour the plaster into the mold so it doesn't move. A Jell-O mold works well too. Before the plaster sets, but when it is firm enough, simply press colorful or interesting stones or shells into the plaster. You'll end up with great textures and colors and a cool thing to hang in the yard or even use as a centerpiece on a picnic table.

Stone pile

THE ART OF STONE PILING. Stone

pilings were used to mark the burial grounds of the Native Americans and other cultures. They were used to mark trails by the same Native Americans as well as the trail blazers who followed. We can still find stone pilings on the Appalachian Trail and others in the United States.

Stone piling is art in its simplest form. It's not far from using simple building blocks to experiment with construction. It may be about looking closely at and appreciating the inherent beauty and wonder of the natural world. And the best part is that it can be a lot of fun.

Stone walls are a form of stone piling. When I first moved to New England I couldn't believe how beautiful some of the old stone walls were. These were made from stone pulled from fields and gardens and built as stone fences. What a lot of effort! Hundreds of years later they are still standing. They're a record of human ingenuity and expression.

Be a Rock Artist

To make your own "rock art," find a location where a stone pile might look nice. You might already have a collection of stones from clearing your garden or helping in the yard.

Stone piling is little more than a balancing act. Take the nice stones you select and see how you can create shapes and forms. The more you try this, the better you'll get at it. Once you think you're finished, step back and take a look. Don't worry if it falls—you can rebuild. And you probably learned something in the process.

Take a picture of your stone pile because these creations don't last forever. Wind or rain or your little brother or sister might knock it down.

If it lasts in the yard, check it out at different times of the day. Watch the changing shadows it casts as the sunlight moves across it from morning to night. Imagine how stone piles were used in ancient times and other cultures. They are often referred to as *cairns*. If you work at it, you can measure the shadows and have a good idea of the time of day.

Start weaving and see what you come up with. Then you can decorate with things like berries or pinecones or feathers.

I recently came across this piling left on the shore of Six Mile Island on Lake Winnepasaukee in New Hampshire.

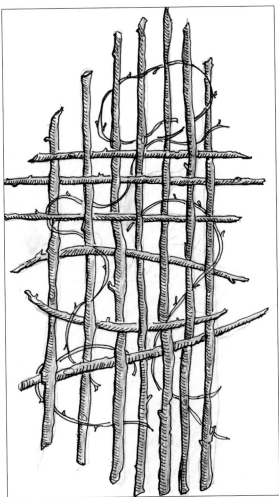

The Art of Stick Weaving

Stick weaving is another ancient art. You can do this in your own yard by collecting thin sticks, about a $\frac{1}{4}$" thick and a few feet long. Collect sticks that have recently fallen and aren't completely dry. Fall is a good season for it. Slightly moist sticks are much easier to bend without breaking. If your sticks snap easily, soak them in warm water to make them easier to bend without breaking. You can make fences out of sticks or artwork to hang on the wall or out in the garden or screened porch. You can make a small border for your garden. Or just have fun trying. This is also a great way to pick up all the sticks out of the lawn.

Grapevine Wreaths

Grapevine wreathes are simple to make. Look for thin vines stems in trees. They are wild and invasive. The best time to gather the stems is in

autumn, when the plants are dormant. It's as simple as cutting vine stems and twisting them into circles (about 30" in diameter). When you get the knack of twisting and tucking the vines into themselves you'll find it pretty easy. Once you like the thickness or mass of the twisted vine, you can decorate it with pinecones or dried flowers.

Simple grapevine wreath

"A shelter of sticks" at the Desert Botanical Garden in Scottsdale, Arizona.

In nature, sticks form their own art.

If you want a great example of this process, take a closer look at birds' nests. There's a picture of a blue jay's nest in Chapter 8.

Painting on Slate or Bluestone

You'll need an old broken piece of bluestone or slate. Wash it off. With chalk, draw a light outline of the simple image you want to paint. The chalk will wash right off when you're finished. And then paint. Try acrylics. Stone art doesn't have to be perfect. It only has to be fun.

Painting on bluestone

 Painting on Wood

Have an unsightly side of the house? Or a barn? Or a storage shed? How about the big side of a garage where nothing will grow? That's the perfect place for your first art show. Outdoor paintings won't last forever, but should last for years and can be a great way to brighten up some dull places in the yard. Look to see if there's a good place to display your talent. If it's a big space you can create a few small paintings like I did on the previous page. Share a big piece (a 4' x 4' piece of plywood, for instance) with a family or friends. Don't be surprised if everyone wants to get involved. We're all artists at heart, after all.

Start small. Take a piece of scrap wood or plywood, or buy a small piece of wood. The ones in the photos are 2' x 2' squares. It's best to lightly sand the edges and put a primer coat on the bare wood before you start to paint. Prime the edges too, especially for plywood because it's made in layers and can peel apart when it's exposed to bad weather. If you prime both sides and the edges, your wood paintings should last several years.

A simple beginner set of acrylic paints or even some leftover house paint will work. Sketch lightly with pencil or chalk, or better yet, do a separate sketch on a piece of paper before you start on the wood. Get a paintbrush or two and a small container of water to wash the brushes off. And then get started and see what you can do. Bright colors show up great in summer and light colors still stand out in the winter.

Wood painting

Part Three:

Fall

GREAT PUMPKINS AND MORE FALL HARVEST FUN

Fall is the season of harvest. One of the greatest reasons to grow plants is to grow food. In Chapter 3 you planned and planted a garden. By fall, you will have already harvested and enjoyed lots of the fruit and vegetables you grew. The most fun fall vegetables include pumpkins and gourds . . . just in time for Halloween.

Carving Pumpkins has become a great tradition in our country for Halloween. It actually started when the first English and Irishmen came over to America and used to carve the pumpkins into lanterns. In Europe, they used to carve turnips. The early American settlers put candles inside of carved pumpkins to provide light.

Pumpkin Carving

Most of us have tried this at Halloween. But there are ways to master the art of pumpkin carving. If you're happy with the triangle eyes and nose, then that's what's important. If you want to try something new, it's time to try some serious carving. You can make hair and eyebrows by carving thin lines halfway through the skin rather than all the way. Any details you create in this way will give your pumpkin a whole new personality.

Of course, you don't have to carve; you can simply paint a face on a pumpkin and set it out for Halloween.

Jack-o-lantern carving

 # Tasty Roasted Pumpkin Seeds

Remove the seeds from the pumpkin, and wash them in a colander. Let the seeds dry and spread them on a baking dish. Sprinkle with salt and drizzle with oil. Bake at 250 degrees for an hour, turning them occasionally. Enjoy! Try adding cinnamon, sugar, or garlic powder in the mix for variety.

And, of course, there's always pumpkin pie . . .

Saving Pumpkin Seeds for Next Year's Garden

You'll get a lot of seeds from a single pumpkin, but only some will germinate next year. Wash them off well and remove all the gooey pulp. Spread them out and put them someplace cool for a week to ten days. Then you can simply put them in an envelope for next spring. In the spring you'll be ready to plant them in the garden in full sun, or start them indoors.

Plants with Spooky Names for the Season

Eyeball Plant

Bloodwort

Ghost Plant

Ghost Fern

Witch Hazel

Wolfsbane

These plants will grow through the summer, and in the fall you can add some of your pumpkins and gourds and the stalks of your harvested corn plants to the Halloween garden.

A Halloween horror

 ## Painting Gourds

You can find some gourds at the local market or grow them yourself and paint different faces on each one. Outline the face in magic marker

first. Use tempera or acrylic paint. Put all the faces in a bowl for Halloween and you might just bowl your friends over with a pot of "shrunken heads." If you have some peat pots and some annual rye seed left, you can grow another crop of googly-eyed people for the Halloween season. Start your rye seeds two weeks before Halloween. (See page 24.)

Spring surprise: A little work in fall pays off in early spring.

114

MORE FALL PLANTING. Fall is a season of

harvest, but it can also be a wonderful planting season for certain plants.

Bulbs (Tulips, Daffodils, Crocuses, Narcissus, and More)

Bulbs are fun to plant, but you won't see any flowers until next spring. The bulbs you plant in the ground are like little storage containers for roots and other things the plants need to grow. Wait until it's getting pretty cold out before you plant the bulbs, because you really don't want them to "wake up" until spring. If it's too early, and it gets warm again before winter, the bulb may sprout but won't flower or do well. You really want to wait until November. Plant the bulbs generally about three times as deep as the height of the bulb (i.e., a 2"-high bulb should

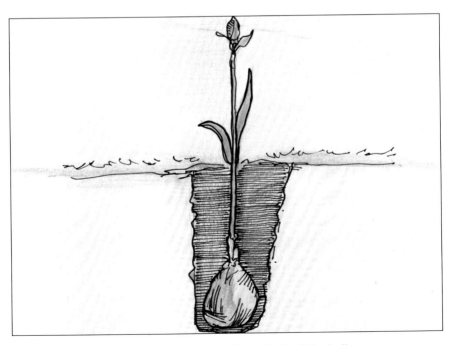

Plant your bulbs at a depth three times the height of the bulb.

be planted in a hole 6" deep). Press gently on the dirt once you've filled the hole to remove air pockets.

Bulbs like daffodils can be quite large, while crocuses and others are very small. Putting some kind of mulch over the top of the planted bulb helps lessen the effects of temperature changes. Cold and snow cover are great for bulbs. Wait until you see them next spring. Even if you forget you planted them, they'll pop up and surprise you.

Enjoy the beautiful blossoms in spring. When the flower's done all that will be left are the tall foliage stalks. Don't cut these back until they begin to brown as this is how the bulb restores itself for another appearance next spring. You can get many springs of enjoyment from a single bulb planting.

Fall Planting: Garlic, Lettuce, and Kale

If you start lettuce or kale seedlings inside in August, you'll be able to plant these out in the garden in September. These will grow well in the cooling weather and can be harvested though the late fall and

early winter. You can also plant kale earlier in the summer. The best kale comes after a frost and even some snow. Most years you can harvest kale into November and some-times even later.

This simple tool makes the job easier.

October is a great time to plant garlic, which is a member of the onion family and a favorite of cooks. Plant the single cloves in full sun with their tips 2" beneath the soil about 5" apart. The cloves will rest dormant (almost like sleeping) for the winter, and the plants will begin to emerge in spring and be ready to harvest in midsummer.

PUTTING THE GARDEN TO BED. Fall

is the best time to get your garden soil ready for next spring. After you've harvested the last of your pumpkins, spread your best compost over the garden. Add fallen leaves to the soil as well.

Add some dried manure (available at stores—unless you have access to cow, horse, or other farm animal manure) and mix this all into the top 5–6" of the garden bed. This will continue to break down over the winter and you'll have a beautiful soil mixture in the spring. It doesn't hurt to leave a few of the old vegetable plants in the garden to degrade and become part of the circle and the rich mix for your spring garden.

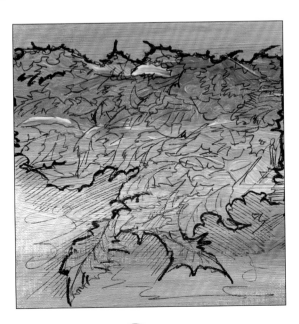

COLD PEAS AND ROTTEN POTATOES: THE JOYS OF COMPOST

Rotten Potatoes? Yuch!

Hold on a minute. Although we may no longer want these with our dinner, they still serve a great purpose. And that's called compost. Composting is one of the great things we can do for our gardens and our world. It's green recycling. **Recycling** is when you take stuff you've used and are going to throw away, and instead make it a part of something that can be used again.

Recycling food scraps is an important part of good composting.

COMPOSTING refers to the process of putting organic material into a storage area where it can break down (decompose) and become rich material (called humus) to be added to the dirt in the garden. The practice of recycling food and other vegetable waste can reduce the amount of trash we send to the landfills or garbage dumps by as much as a third. And it is just like the recycling that happens in nature, when leaves drop to the ground and become part of the dirt. It's your small circle that mimics the big circle of natural life.

Here are some of the things you can add to the compost pile while cleaning the yard: old leaves, cut grass, weeds, and plants that you no longer want in the garden; scraps from fruit and vegetables; the finished plants from your vegetable garden and any fruit or vegetable you didn't get to eat; tea bags and coffee grounds; and, of course, cold peas and rotten potatoes.

Making Your Own
Simple Compost Bin

You can buy pre-made compost bins that are neat and attractive. Some of them even turn with a handle so the compost is regularly turned over. These are called "compost tumblers." But making a starter compost bin is

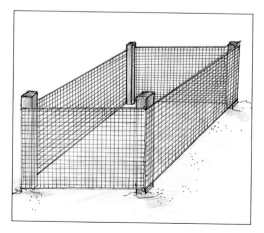

easy. Here's a simple diagram and instructions.

The simplest way to make a compost bin is to pick up some wooden stakes. 5–6' high and 2" x 2". (If you want to build a nicer-looking compost bin as part of your gardens and

Simple compost bin

landscape, you can use 4' x 4' cedar posts as the anchor posts. Using these posts enable you to put hooks on the posts so you can actually remove the screening material if you want.

Find a space that gets at least a few hours of sun per day and is away from where you spend most of your time in the yard, but still convenient from the house or kitchen. Measure a rectangle large enough for your compost; anywhere from 2' x 4' or 3' x 6'. Make it narrow enough so you can reach into the center with a pitchfork to turn things over once in a while. Drive the stakes into the ground deep enough so they're sturdy. Purchase some thin gauge wire (vinyl coated is better because it won't rust) and staple or nail it to the stakes. A height of 3' works well so you can reach over it easily. You can leave one side tied off lightly so it can be opened to shovel or pitchfork compost out of the bin.

It's best to fill the compost bin in layers and then mix things up every few weeks. A pitchfork or baling fork is great for this. Water the layers in hot and dry periods.

Good layering helps compost.

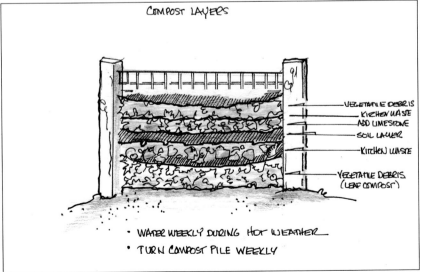

Part Four:

Winter

13

TO SNOW AND BEYOND

If you live in a place where it snows in winter, everything becomes covered in a blanket of white. Winter brings us a soft and quiet world. Having some snow cover through a cold winter actually helps plants. It insulates the ground from the worst cold and protects the roots and some of the important lower **foliage** (leaves) from the winter wind.

As your garden sleeps, a snowy yard can be a wonderful playground full of fun projects to hold you over until you can start planting seeds again.

A SHOUT OUT ABOUT SPROUTS: GROWING SPROUTS IN WINTER FOR FUN AND FOOD.

Sprouts are simply new seed growth. They contain a lot of vitamins and nutrients. Seeds that are good for sprouting include beans, peas, broccoli, sunflowers, radishes, and many more. You can also buy sprouting mixes that contain different kinds of seeds that all sprout well. You'll simply need to soak the seeds overnight and place them in a glass container without soil. Rinse and

Another approach to sprouts, as demonstrated by Molly: Soak the seeds overnight. Put a teaspoon of seaweed fertilizer in trays, fill the trays with potting soil and dampen the soil. Spread the seeds on the surface of the soil. Cover lightly with wet newspaper four or five sheets thick. Put in a dark closet for four days. Check to make sure newspaper doesn't dry out. On fourth day, sprouts should be lifting newspaper. Take out of the dark, remove newspaper, then water and put in sun for three to four more days to green up and allow to grow taller. Cut with scissors at base and eat! Compost the leftover soil and roots.

drain well daily and within a few days you'll see the white sprouts growing. Soon they'll fill the jar. Put the jar on a sunny sill and they will turn green. Once you have enough sprouts to harvest, they're great on sandwiches or in a salad or just plain, eaten out of the jar.

WINDOW GARDENS. There are some plants that
will do well inside in the winter. If you have a window that is available, you can build a shelf or set some plants on a tall table. Try plants that like sun. African violets do very well in an eastern exposure (morning sun) and bloom throughout the year.

A window with full southern sun exposure is a good place to try a cactus garden. You can purchase sandy soil and a low container and establish some cactus plants, called succulents. Add rocks and make your own miniature desert.

There are also bulbs you can grow inside in winter. Look for "paperwhites" or large Amaryllis bulbs. Amaryllis bulbs are usually available in a kit. They are a giant bulb that comes

in a box. Set on a windowsill, water, and watch it grow. Paper-whites are smaller bulbs and can be set in a sunny window in a bowl of stone and water and they'll produce beautiful, fragrant flowers in weeks.

Winter Whites: fragrant blossoms in a sunny window.

SNOW AND ICE SCULPTURE.

If there are at least 6" of snow on the ground and you've had enough of sledding and snowboarding, it's time to discover your inner artist and take it into the outer winter world.

You've probably made a snowman or two. So how about you take it up a notch. Snow and ice sculptures are world-renowned art forms. But the process is simple. It really just requires some snow and a little creativity. The snow is outside and you're the creative one.

The famous sculptor Michelangelo claimed that he would chisel away at the stone until he found the figure inside. Well, that's a cool idea (or should I say cold?) to consider when you think about making forms out of snow.

You can look at the piles of snow and see shapes within. Or you can shovel and roll up your own piles and make whatever shape you like. Part of the fun is doing our own personal thing.

Getting Started

You need snow and temperatures between twenty and thirty degrees. Too warm and snow gets mushy. Too cold and it gets icy.

Bundle up and go out on a sunny day. Wear waterproof gloves and get some hot chocolate or tea ready for when you get back inside.

Tools:

Snow shovel or something like it

Hand trowel

Old spoon

Small container for water (use warm water so it takes longer to freeze)

Optional:

If you want to carve some detail (like whiskers or wrinkles) you'll need some smaller hand tools. Try an old spatula or putty knife.

If you want to take it one step further and add some color:

Clear plastic container

Food coloring that can be mixed with snow to create a colored shush that you can work with

Choose a Model:

If you're a beginner, choose something simple for the first try. How about a favorite stuffed animal? A dog or a cat? Work from a picture or something else. And there's nothing wrong with an old-fashioned snowman.

Making Frozen Eyes and Other Features, Such as Ice Cubes:

If you want to get fancy, ice cubes colored with food coloring can make eyes and other features. Simply fill an ice tray with the colored water of your choice and put it in the freezer. Carve out holes for eye sockets and insert your colored ice cubes.

Wing It:

It's okay to just start shaping and carving and see what emerges. There's no wrong in snow shaping.

Sculpting

Use a shovel to make a packed mound of snow or tamp down an existing one.

Start from the top so you can be sure to keep the bottom wide enough to support the top.

Remove excess snow with a small shovel to make the basic shape of your subject.

During the process, if you make a mistake, have a small pail with water nearby. Use the warm water to erase any snow mistakes. Mix a little snow with a little water to make a kind of a paste. Work it into the area and let it freeze, then start again or continue on.

Now you're ready to get going on your work of art. And the best thing about creating art is that if you like it, then it's great.

WARNING: Do not get too attached to your new snow sculpture. Take photos and enjoy them while they last and create a new one next time you have snow.

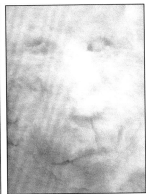

Snow Measuring Sticks

Take a square stake 2" x 2" and 5–6' tall. Drive the stake into the ground 8–12" so it will stay upright. (You need to do this before the ground freezes hard.) Measure off 6" increments and mark them with a pencil or magic marker. Then paint each increment a different color. Write down what color indicates what depth. In winter you should be able to look out of the window and see your stake. If it's yellow, it might be 6" deep. Maybe blue is 3" deep.

Snow measuring stick

Wind Sock

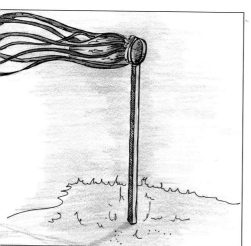

Take a thin plastic bag, like the ones you get from the grocery store, or a small laundry hosiery bag. Staple some light plastic ribbon or colorful yarn to the bag. Different colored ribbons make a nice show on a windy day.

Cut out a 2" plastic ring from a quart-size plastic bottle.

Tape or staple the opening of the bag, ribbons and all, to the plastic ring.

Drive a small stake into the ground and leave it about 4' high (tomato stakes will work nicely).

Nail the plastic ring to the top of the stake, leaving it loose enough to spin. It should droop down if it's not windy and take off like a flag when it is. The plastic will spin and the ribbons will follow, which will point in the direction of the wind when they are in full stream. It'll tell you about the wind direction and intensity, and look pretty cool in the yard.

It won't last forever, but it's easy to make and you can invent your own variations.

Weather Journal

Start a weather journal. Winter's a great time to put your information together in a scrapbook. We've already measured rain and snow. And you can observe the wind direction with your wind sock. Keep notes, photos, or sketches in your journal and revisit them each winter.

GREETINGS THAT GROW—HOW TO MAKE YOUR OWN PAPER. A garden

in the mail? This is one of the coolest things you can do to surprise friends and family, while jumping on that merry-go-round of seasons and recycling. Did you know you could give or receive a greeting card that will grow a garden? Well you can and this chapter shows you how.

Paper is made from wood. The wood is ground up and water is added and everything is mushed up into something called pulp. Pulp looks like lumpy mashed potatoes.

Since paper comes from trees, it's important that we plant enough new trees to replace the ones we use for paper. And there are many new laws in this country that make sure this happens most of the time. But you can recycle paper in your own kitchen. And you can make nice thick paper out of recycled wrapping paper and newspaper. You can add color too.

 # Make Your Own Paper

What you'll need:

Old paper

A bowl or container

Blender or food processor (it's nice if you have an older one you can use just for this purpose)

Water

Food coloring (optional)

An old window screen

A picture frame or some kind of frame that will determine the size of your paper

Sponge

Cut old recycled paper (any kind of paper) into strips or shred it if you have a shredder. Put it in a bowl with an equal amount of water. Put the mixture in a blender and blend it until it's a thick pulp. Add food coloring if you want color. A tablespoon of cornstarch makes it easier to write on the paper.

You can use an old window screen or buy some screen and make your own screener. Place the screen over a sink or tub. Set the picture frame on top of your screen. Pour the pulp into the picture frame. The pulp will take the shape and size of the picture frame. Press it gently down with a sponge. Press out all the water you can through the screen. Then turn the pulp mass over on aluminum foil or a cookie sheet. Place newspaper over the pressed pulp to remove excess moisture. Add flower petals or small leaves to the pulp, if you like. When the pulp dries, it will be a nice thick paper that will fold into a greeting card.

 # Adding Decorations

You can add food coloring to some of the pulp and put it all back in the blender again. Now remove the new colored pulp and form a shape with it using cookie cutters as forms, or form new shapes by hand and press the shape onto the greeting card before it dries.

Adding Seeds

Now that you've learned how to make your own homemade paper, here's the next step. Before you finish spreading the new paper out on its frame, add seeds to the mix. The seeds will stay alive for months. Let the person receiving it know that they can plant it right in the ground in the spring! The paper will rot away and compost and the seeds will grow into whatever flower, herb, or vegetable you decided to include. That card you made will grow.

Greetings that grow

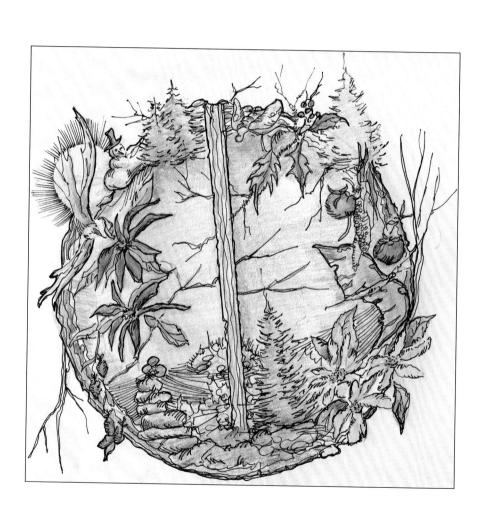

14

WHAT GOES AROUND COMES AROUND

Ending at the beginning—beginning at the end. A big circle, right? Once winter reaches a peak in late January and February, spring is right around the corner. Remember to look out for seed catalogs. It's almost that time again. The snow is melting or at least beginning to melt. The ground is beginning to thaw and getting a little mushy and muddy. That's the real sign of spring. February's a short month. March can't always decide whether it's part of winter or spring. But it always turns to April. And then you know what they say about April showers? They bring May flowers. Giant sunflowers and popcorn gardens and pumpkins are just around the corner. And now, you'll have a pile of cold peas and rotten potatoes to add to your garden as compost. Only this year, you might have grown some of them yourself.

Somewhere the butterflies and bugs are stirring. Birds are considering a return to your yard and garden. Plants that have been asleep for winter are beginning to stretch their roots, looking for water and nutrients. The winter blanket is being pulled back to reveal another spring. Perhaps somewhere in the garden those bulbs you planted in the fall are just starting to pop and thrust themselves upward through the good soil to the sun and the rain and become tulips and crocuses and beautiful daffodils.

It's time to start planning your spring and summer garden. Sketch out ideas. Get those peat pots ready. This year you're more experienced. And if you've followed the seasons through the chapters of this book, you're already well on your way to being a gardener or a landscaper. You know nature is a giant circle, and now you're an active part of the unbroken cycle of the seasons. So, get dirty and have fun!